How to Turn the Other Cheek and Still Survive in Today's World

Suzette Haden Elgin

A JANET THOMA BOOK

THOMAS NELSON PUBLISHERS
Nashville • Atlanta • London • Vancouver

Published in Nashville, Tennessee, by Thomas Nelson, Inc. Publishers, and distributed in Canada by Word Communications, Ltd., Richmond, British Columbia, and in the United Kingdom by Word (UK), Ltd., Milton Keynes, England.

Scripture quotations are from the NEW KING JAMES VERSION of the Bible. Copyright © 1979, 1980, 1982, Thomas Nelson, Inc., Publishers.

Library of Congress Cataloging-in-Publication Data

Elgin, Suzette Haden.
    How to turn the other cheek and still survive in today's world / Suzette Haden Elgin.
    Includes bibliographical references and index.
    ISBN 0-7852-7249-6 (pbk.)
    1. Verbal self-defense. 2. Interpersonal communication. 3. Interpersonal conflict. 4. Verbal self-defense—Religious aspects—Christianity.
    5. Interpersonal communication—Religious aspects—Christianity.
    6. Interpersonal conflict—Religious aspects—Christianity. I. Title
    BF637.V47E4315   1997
    153.6—dc21   97-20697
                                                                  CIP

Printed in the United States of America
1 2 3 4 5 6 7 QPK 03 02 01 00 99 98 97

CONTENTS

ACKNOWLEDGMENTS

For this book, I am most deeply indebted to all the men and women who, over the past twenty-five years, have posed questions for me about resolving the seeming conflict between the rules of business and the commandments of their faith. I thank each and every one of them for the clarity and deep-felt passion of their questions, which have made it possible for me to see exactly where the problems are, and how those problems intersect with language.

I am also grateful to the many scholars whose work has provided the foundation upon which my work has been built. Special thanks are due to Dr. Owen Clayton, whose extraordinary theological insight and learning have been so generously shared with me. I am grateful to my editors at Thomas Nelson—and especially to Janet Thoma—for guiding me through the writing and production of this book; they have been astonishingly patient with me.

Finally, my thanks go as always to my long-suffering family, whose love and support make what I do possible. Responsibility for mistakes and omissions is, of course, entirely mine.

Suzette Haden Elgin, Ph.D.

INTRODUCTION

> You have heard that it was said, "An eye for
> an eye and a tooth for a tooth." . . . But who-
> ever slaps you on your right cheek, turn the
> other to him also.
>
> Matthew 5:38–39

My client and I were discussing the difference between direct and indirect commands (not a highly emotional topic!) when he—the top executive of a successful company, a confident husband and father, a leader of church and civic groups, and a pillar of his community—suddenly began falling apart before my eyes. We'd been working together only briefly, but I knew already that he wasn't a man who wept or asked for help easily; he was doing both of those things now. I also knew that the grammatical point we'd been discussing couldn't possibly be the source of his distress. I reminded him that I'm not a therapist, but he raised his hand to hush me, and shook his head.

"I have to talk to you about this," he said, his voice hoarse and shaking. "Because I believe you will understand, and because I think you may have some ideas that will help."

"I'm listening," I told him, and I gave him my full and careful attention. I was reasonably sure I knew what was coming next, and I was not mistaken.

"We were talking," he said, "about the way I use language— and how the way I give commands often makes the people who work for me **resentful**. And I have to explain to you **why** I handle that so badly! Dr. Elgin, what my employees hear in my voice that makes them uneasy about trusting me is my **shame**. Shame! Because, you know what I do? I go around talking, even giving speeches, about running a Christian business; where I live, I'm the person they call on for speeches like that. I get up in front of people, and I say all the right things, and they clap ... but **half** of what I say is **lies**, and even when I speak the truth I don't practice it in my own life. The fact is, it's not **possible** to run an American business by Christian principles today—it can't be **done!** I am such a hypocrite that I can't stand myself any longer. I can't walk out on my faith, and I can't walk out on my family or my business, and the only way on earth I can keep all three going at once is by living a perpetual lie ... and I tell you frankly, I do not know what to **do!**"

He cleared his throat then and apologized for making a speech at *me*.

"It's all right," I assured him. "I've heard that particular speech hundreds of times, in one version or another, over the years. I've heard it from businesspeople, teachers, parents, clergy, from every sort of person. Please believe me—you're not *alone* with that lie, my friend, or with your problem." And that was and still is true.

The Problem We Face

We need to be very frank here, right from the beginning, because continuing to tiptoe around this issue will only add to it still more layers of confusion and misunderstanding. Wading into icy water one inch at a time makes the misery far worse and more long-lasting; we all know that. Let's apply that knowledge and dive headfirst into the icy waters of this question.

Ask almost any rational adult in our society what he or she thinks of the quotation that opened this chapter. If the answer is truthful, it will go something like this: "In the context of today's world, it seems completely unacceptable; in fact, if it had any other source I'd call it *nonsense*!"

Why? Consider what the quotation appears to mean:

Suppose you are a child, and the class bully knocks you down on the playground. That quotation says you can't hit him back; you can't tell the teacher or your parents what he did so he'll be stopped and perhaps punished; you can't call him names. You can't do *anything* to him; you have to turn the other cheek!

Suppose you're an adult, walking home, bothering no one, and a couple of thugs come along and knock *you* down—your options are the same as the child's. Can you hit back? Can you tell the thugs off? Can you call the police and have them taken away to jail? No. You, like the child, have to turn the other cheek.

Suppose you're in business, and one of your customers refuses to pay your bill for goods already delivered. According to the quoted verses, you can't go to the customer and take your goods back. You can't call the other businesspeople you know and warn them against the customer. You can't sue her in a court of law. You can't even refuse to sell to her again. You have to turn the other cheek.

Isn't this nonsense?

It gets worse. Elsewhere in the Bible, the command is expanded, ordering you not only to turn that cheek but to return good for the evil done to you. Certainly, turning the other cheek instead of bashing someone *is* good returned for evil, in the sense of refraining from what might be done, but it's not enough. Just refraining won't do it—you have to *act*. You are commanded to love your enemies, to bless those who curse you, to do good to those who hate you. The child or adult who is abused by a bully or a thug, physically or in any other way, is supposed to invite the abuser home for a good meal. The businessperson is supposed to send the cheating customer an offer for a bigger discount!

This *is* what the verses appear to say, and we all know it. No matter what nuances they may contain for scholars of Greek and

Hebrew and Aramaic, this is the meaning the rest of us have to come to terms with, and this is the problem we're up against every day of our lives. As has rightly been said, the "eleventh" commandment is, "You do, too, know what I mean."

Trusting God is the foundation of faith and the beginning of the spiritual life. But how can there be trust in the face of a command to do the impossible? After all, the verses don't say, "*Try* to do this*," they command it without reservation or qualification. It's as if a parent said to a child, in absolute seriousness: "Disobey me!" We would rightly call that both cruel and perverse, since the child can obey only by *dis*obeying and the contradiction can't be resolved. Surely, at minimum we have to know that God will never *order* us to do what can't be done! What, then, are we to make of this "turning the other cheek" business?

A number of traditional ways to wiggle out of such quandaries exist:

- Sometimes we can say that the command was meant entirely for another day and age, like the verses in Leviticus ordering people who have touched the carcass of a lobster to go wash their clothes.
- Sometimes we can say that an error has been made in the translation, as with the famous "voice of the turtle" in the Song of Solomon. We now know that voice belongs to a turtle *dove*.
- Sometimes we can claim that a particular sequence "doesn't really mean what it says," though we usually try not to put it that bluntly. For example, we may say that the two meanings involved in the translation are so different that confusion is unavoidable—as with Matthew 5:48, where Jesus says flatly that "You shall be perfect." Not "you *will* be," which we might take as a prediction or a promise, but "you

shall be," which is unmistakably a command. Scholars commenting on that verse tell us that *perfect* in English is untranslatably different from the *perfect* of the biblical language, and that we are not *really* being ordered to be perfect, not in the English sense of the word.

- And there are times when we can fall back on the claim that the difficult verse is simply so mysterious that we have to set it aside and trust that we'll be able to figure it out in the afterlife. "Farther along, we'll know all about it."

None of these wiggles is going to work when it comes to the instruction to turn the other cheek. Even if one or more of them applied, we'd still have to face the problem, because there are so many *backup* verses offering us clarification in case we didn't get it the previous time! The Bible is filled with them. Love your neighbor the way you love yourself, it says. Do to others what you'd want them to do to you, it says. Love those who hate you, it says, and when they do you wrong, do them good. Many things in the Bible may justly be called difficult and obscure, but *this* one is made abundantly clear: Revenge and retribution belong not to us but to God, and *we* are ordered to turn the other cheek! *Case closed.* As my despairing client wanted to know: What are we to *do*?

I am not a religious expert; I would not presume to write about religious doctrine. Where this same dilemma runs us up against tremendous issues like the death penalty and euthanasia, I would not attempt even to comment. I leave such matters to the theologians and clergy. But my client was right—I do know some useful things that are applicable to many aspects of this problem and that can go a long way toward solving it at least in our everyday lives.

For the past quarter of a century I have been writing and speaking and teaching about verbal violence and verbal self-defense. I explain to my readers and listeners that verbal violence is where physical violence *begins*, and that hostile language—even when it doesn't escalate to physical force—is toxic. I explain that poisonous language is as dangerous as any other kind of poison and that our environment today is contaminated with it in a way that is destroying our lives and crippling our souls. I explain that by the grace of God we human beings are superbly equipped to *avoid* such language and to defend ourselves against it—and I explain how that is done. And during all these years I have had a steady flood of questions like these from my audiences and readers:

- "Sure, I know the Bible says a soft answer turns away wrath! But you can't just let people walk all **over** you! How can you do that 'soft answer' stuff without everybody seeing you as a hopeless WIMP? How can you expect people to have any **respect** for you?"
- "Everybody else is running their businesses by the rule of 'do evil unto others before **they** do evil unto **you**!' Suppose I try to follow the Golden Rule . . . How can I even hold my own, much less COMPETE?"
- "All this 'love your enemies' stuff sounds great in church, but what use is it in the real world? Do you know what would happen to me and my family and my business if I went around loving my enemies and doing good to them? Listen, it's a **jungle** out there!"
- "Yeah, we're supposed to be slow to anger, we're supposed to forgive seventy times seven, we're supposed to return good for evil—but we're also expected to take care of ourselves and our families! Come on—HOW can that be possible? It's riDICulous!"

- "I get up in the morning and I look at myself in the mirror," they all tell me, "and what I see looking back at me is a **hypocrite.** How am I supposed to live with that? But if I do what the Bible says, how am I supposed to live at ALL???"

As the tattered cliché puts it, *I feel the pain these people feel*, and I address that pain by telling them it's time to take another long and extremely careful look at what's really going on here. Because much of our pain has its source not in our faith or in our values, not in our weaknesses or our strengths, but in our language. And that *is* my area of expertise; that—because I am a linguist—I can help with.

Let me give you now the very basic example with which our exploration and discussion has to begin.

MARCHING—GENTLY— AS TO WAR?

Obviously, we Christian people today do not admire (and we refuse to live by) the model of the "gentle Jesus, meek and mild." That's clear. And what metaphor have we chosen instead? You can find the answer to that question by looking on the shelves of any religious bookstore. We have not chosen the Shepherd or even the Parent; overwhelmingly, our chosen model for both men and women is the Warrior. Warriors are *not* meek and mild. Warriors are brave, loyal, honest, trustworthy, and strong. They stand up for their principles; they defend their country and their home and their loved ones. They stand firm for freedom and truth. You can put your hand in a Warrior's hand and go confidently forward, knowing that you are safe—because whatever may happen, the Warrior will be able to deal with it.

But look carefully at that *word*, please! *Warrior.* What does it mean, to you?

In his book, *Tender Warrior,* Stu Weber writes that "There is a difference between a warrior and a brute" (1993, 41). No doubt there is; but our culture perceives that difference as primarily a difference of *skill.* When we speakers of English look at the word *warrior,* we see *war,* plus one of the English endings for *doer.* Our language tells us that a preacher is one who preaches, an actor is one who acts—and a warrior is one who *wars.* When we go to any movie with "Warrior" prominently featured in its title, we expect to see a hero who hits and overpowers and maims and, if necessary, kills. *That's what* Warrior *means.* We do not expect to see that hero turning the other cheek and returning good for evil. When we say or hear the word, when we read or write it, when we think it, this is how we understand it. Putting *spiritual* in front of *warrior* (or *warfare*) doesn't make it mean something else; our minds don't work that way, where language is concerned.

Someone could certainly declare that a teacher is a person who *swims.* Someone powerful might be able to force us to pretend that we agree with that. But whenever we watch a skillful teacher in action and say, "Now **that's** what I call good **swimming!**" we would be lying. Our minds would not be changed. It is just as difficult to get the *war* out of *warrior* as it is to get the *teach* out of *teacher.* And who ever heard of a gentle war? Who ever heard of a war in which the warriors loved their enemies and did their best to be good to them? Who ever sang a hymn about Christian soldiers marching gently and meekly and tenderly off to war?

We live in a world where, despite the fact that the Bible commands us more than twenty times to do things gently, gentleness is despised. I know this very well indeed; I am reminded of it constantly in my work. The system I teach is called "the gentle art of verbal self-defense," but many of my clients insist that I leave the "gentle" out of my seminar title. Why? "Because our doctors [*nurses, employees, teachers, members*] won't come to a seminar with that word in its name!" Every part of our society appears to support these three propositions:

1. Winning is everything.
2. Losing is a disgrace.
3. And we, we Warriors, are obligated to get out there and *fight*.

This is the heart of our difficulty, and this is where the misery begins—as we devote ourselves to the ethic of the Warrior and strive to behave like one, while at the same time believing that we are commanded to behave totally *unlike* a Warrior. If we are honest, we have to admit that our model and metaphor for turning the other cheek is the *Coward*.

We don't like to say that, but it is the truth. In our minds, we see it like this: The Warrior strikes the cringing Coward across the face, presumably for excellent reasons; the Coward then offers the other cheek in a desperate effort to placate and escape. Our culture—even the parts looked upon as spiritual—keeps insisting that we must be the Warrior. The Bible seemingly orders us to be the Coward. Desperately, we keep trying to find some way to meet both demands at the same time.

In this way lies a kind of religious schizophrenia, a sort of grid-lock of the spirit and mind. We cannot be both Warrior and Coward at the same time. That really *is* impossible. And the very idea that God commands us to be Cowards is intolerable! There are no books on the shelves titled *How to Be A Coward for Christ* or *Thirty Days to Spiritual Cowardice*. And after all, didn't Jesus say, in the very same Bible, that He was *not* here to bring peace?

When we human beings find ourselves in a situation like this, facing the unfaceable, we tend to choose one course of action and stick to it doggedly, no matter how badly things go. We are like a person digging a well and finding no water, who goes on endlessly making the same dry hole deeper and deeper instead of digging somewhere else.

We are making two basic errors here over and over again, errors not of faith but of language, that condemn us to this gridlock:

1. We have misunderstood the instruction to turn the other cheek, and we keep trying to make that misunderstanding fit, somehow, into our spiritual lives.
2. We have chosen the word *warrior* to name our model and metaphor for the spiritual life, in spite of the fact that the meaning we understand that word to have is totally in conflict with our understanding of the command to turn the other cheek.

It's not surprising that this doesn't work. You need only look at it through the lens of common sense to see that the rational reaction to such a mess is to throw up your hands, say "This is **ridic**ulous!", and go do something else entirely. It is evidence for both the miraculous strength of human faith and the absurd power of human habit that we go on struggling with it as we do.

The first step out of this dilemma is to set aside all our preconceptions, all our fixed ideas and habitual conclusions, about that event in which Person A strikes Person B and Person B turns the other cheek. We have been told, remember, that unless we become as children, we cannot enter the kingdom of God; in the manner of children, we have to reconsider this event as if it were entirely new.

Our reaction up to now—our *adult* reaction—has been, "It can't be true that I have to turn the other cheek when someone strikes me; that's ridiculous. But because the words were spoken by Jesus, I have to **pretend** that I believe those words and will obey them."

This strategy is familiar to all of us because we learned it as small children. We've had lots of practice at it, and we have an accurate name for it: We call it "paying lip service." Remember? Your parents had told you solemnly, over and over, that you must not lie. But when your neighbor came visiting with a new baby and asked you, "Isn't she beautiful?" your mother and father lied and said yes, *right in front of you*! And when you said—truthfully—"She's not beautiful, she's UGly!" you were punished for your honesty. From incidents like this, you learned that you were expected to *pretend* that lying is forbidden and to *pretend* that you would always obey that rule, but that in the real world things are handled differently. And you did your best, given those difficult circumstances.

We have been dealing with "turn the other cheek" in exactly the same way. We've been assuming that turning the other cheek is another such example because somewhere in our distant past we decided that it delivers this message:

"OW! That **hurt**! But it's safe to hit me again, because I'm a **cow-ard** and I'm so **scared** of you! Here, I'll even turn my other cheek toward you so it's more **convenient** for you to hit me!"

I suggest to you that that was a mistake and that turning the other cheek is intended to deliver this *very different* message:

"Please notice—I am not afraid of you at all."

This is no cowardly message! On the contrary, it's strong and serene and confident and unafraid. We have been misunderstanding, all along, in spite of the fact that we trust God not to be perverse, and in spite of the fact that nowhere is there any evidence that Jesus was a coward. The misunderstanding has become so embedded in our culture and our minds, by habit and repetition, that it has hidden the *true* meaning from us all along. To understand how this could have happened, we need to look at three basic linguistic facts.

- It is a basic fact about our language that more than half of *all* information, and more than 90 percent of all *emotional* information, is carried not by our words but by our body language.

Whenever all we have to go on is written language, when we can't see the speaker's face and body or hear the speaker's voice, the chances for misunderstanding multiply. The more difficult the concept being expressed is, and the more conflict there is between that concept and ideas we already hold, the more likely misunderstanding of written language becomes. And in the case of this particular Speaker, all we have had available, for many, many generations, *is* the written language. Even when we are listening to someone read the written language aloud to us, we have only the *reader's* body language, not that of the Speaker.

- It is also a basic linguistic fact that the two acts involved here—striking a person across the face, and turning the other cheek in response to a blow across the face—are not *words*. They are *language* because they communicate a message, but they are units of *body* language.

Words (and phrases made up of words) often have extremely specific meanings. Almost without exception, English speakers in their right minds will agree on the meaning of *table* and *book* and *cup* and *St. Louis, Missouri* and many thousands more. Body language—nonverbal communication—is different. Despite the things you read in popular books on the subject, there are only a very few units of body language that have a single, specific meaning, like the "thumbs-up" gesture that indicates approval in English. Most body language is open to several or many interpretations, based on the words that go with it, the people involved, and the real world context. We have been assuming that the sequence of striking a blow and responding to the blow by turning the other cheek has only one possible meaning and delivers only one possible message, so that there's no reason to look any further. This is an unfortunate confusion of the way *words* work with the way *body* language works.

- It is a basic linguistic fact that every language interaction is a feedback loop. Person A strikes Person B. If Person B strikes back, Person A is now the one forced to choose a proper response. The dilemma of turning the other cheek moves from person to person in turn, for as long as either one returns *evil* for evil.

We should have looked at the two verses and reasoned like this: "These words appear to order me to be a craven coward and a hopeless weakling. But they come from God, whom I trust and honor. Therefore, they must mean something else, and I need to consider the other possibilities." We haven't been doing that, which is a mistake. But does anything other than habit stand in the way of our doing so *now*?

Only one thing. To turn the other cheek to the one who strikes us with the message that "I am not afraid of you at all," we have to *mean* it. We can't just pretend. We have to have the serenity and the confidence and the courage that make the message *true*.

We have to know that no matter what happens, we do have the resources and skills necessary to deal with it—so that we have no *reason* to be afraid. Otherwise, we won't be able to follow through.

That is what this book is about; I am going to show you how you can have—not *pretend* to have, but *really* have—those resources and skills.

We're not hermits, you know, and most of us aren't monks or nuns. We don't live in isolation, we live out in the world. We aren't able to issue occasional written statements and remain otherwise loftily silent. We don't have the luxury of being able to ignore the messages of others. We're lawyers and waitresses, teachers and carpenters, police officers and mechanics and computer programmers; we're politicians and truck drivers and homemakers and military personnel. We're spouses and parents, children and relatives and friends, employers and employees. We have to spend our time doing our best to fulfill our own obligations and achieve our own goals, not in isolation but *in constant interaction with vast numbers of other people who are all trying to do the same thing*.

This makes our task complicated, but it doesn't make it impossible. It makes it more *likely* that we'll keep finding ourselves in situations where blows (literal ones or figurative ones) are struck and where responses to blows are required, but it does not mean that we're helpless to avoid such situations and to avoid them honorably. We will take it one small step at a time, and I will show you how it can be done; we will do it together.

AND WHAT IF
YOU'RE NOT A SAINT?

I want to reassure you about one barrier to turning the other cheek that remains even when we understand it correctly as a message of courage and confidence: your natural suspicion that doing so will only mean substituting the Saint for the Coward. We would all agree that being saintly is a big improvement over being cowardly, but that makes the substitution no less alarming.

Our original misunderstanding had us trapped in an impossible situation much like that of the child who has been told, "Disobey me!" That's gone now. But although you know saintliness isn't impossible, you're unlikely to believe it will be *easy* always to respond with "Notice—I'm not afraid of you at all" instead of "Get your cotton-picking hands OFF me, you CREEP!" (or its equivalent in blows or lawsuits or firings or other demonstrations of anger, power, and resistance).

Stay with me. I promise you that the solutions I present in this book won't require you to be saintly. (If you *can* be, I congratulate you, of course.) Saintliness would be nice, but it most emphatically is not required. All you need is your God-given competence in your native language, your common sense, and a determination to succeed.

HOW TO USE THIS BOOK

This introduction has set out the problem that we need to solve. It will have made clear to you what a linguist's approach to such matters is like. The rest of the book will teach you a set of seven *interacting* language techniques that are practical, easy to use, and have been thoroughly tested in the real world. Although these techniques are based on contemporary linguistic science, they are easily understood and learned. And they are the key to putting into practice in your life the principle of turning the other cheek, without sacrificing your principles or compromising your beliefs—or facing the formidable task of becoming a saint.

Each core chapter has four main parts:

1. A scenario in which ordinary people find themselves involved in a common communication dilemma: a situation in which Person A has to deliver a negative message—a potential verbal slap—and Person B must react and respond to that message. These situations require one or all of the persons who are involved either to turn the other cheek or to find an alternative solution. As can be expected in those circumstances, the scenarios show you people who, often despite the best of intentions, become involved in communication errors, communication breakdowns, and the moral quandaries that result from both.

2. A section that introduces one of the language techniques, explaining it carefully and thoroughly.

3. A return to the scenario, revising and rewriting it to show you how use of the language technique just presented would have made it possible to avoid the conflict and other unfortunate aspects of the original version.

4. A workout section with a variety of practice activities and other information that will supplement the chapter and provide you with opportunities to expand your knowledge base and hone your new skills.

You may want to read through the entire book quickly to gain an overall understanding of its content and then return to the workout sections during a second, more leisurely, reading. Alternatively, you may prefer to stop at the end of each chapter and do the workouts as you go along. Different people have different learning styles—either method is fine.

If you find that you want to read more about some item, you can turn to the References and Bibliography on pages 215–219 to locate appropriate materials. If you realize that you've lost track of some previously encountered term or concept, you can turn to the index at the back of the book and it will direct you to the exact page you need.

Throughout the book I will be using punctuation in a way that may strike you as unusual. Standard English punctuation is almost useless for telling us what sort of tune the words are set to, but we need that information to tell us whether the words are hostile. Look at these three sentences, all containing the same exact words:

1. "Why are you leaving?"
2. "**Why** are you **leaving**?"
3. "**WHY** are **YOU LEAV**ing?!"

The first example is neutral; the questioner just wants to know why you're leaving. Examples 2 and 3, however aren't neutral; now the questioner has an additional *emotional* message to deliver. Example 2 tells us that the questioner is uneasy or distressed in some way; Example 3's questioner is openly hostile. And we understand these differences of meaning only because of the extra emphasis—called *stress*—placed on words or parts of words in the second and third examples.

In quoted speech in this book I will use boldface and capital letters in this way, to help me indicate not just what the speaker is saying but *how* he or she is saying it. And I will use double question marks, double exclamation marks (and even combinations of the two) for the same purpose—to help me sing the tunes with written language.

Above all, take your time with this book, and don't become discouraged. Habits of a lifetime aren't easily discarded. Learning something new *does* take time. Your language isn't new to you—it's one thing for which you need no expert, because you *are* the expert. But I'll be asking you to think about language, and about its use, in ways that may be entirely unfamiliar to you. Don't let that disturb you. I will make it all clear, I promise you. And I'll be with you every step of the way.

Let's get started.

WORKOUT SECTION

1. When you have to go somewhere dangerous, it's helpful to know in advance what the terrain is like, where the dangers are located, when the hazards are most severe, and so on. Nobody wants to walk into danger totally unprepared! Before we go on, then, let's take time to find out how dangerous your own personal language environment is: Is it really "a jungle out there" for you? Your answers to the questions below will give you the basic information about the verbal slaps in your life. (I'd recommend doing this survey on sheets of ruled notebook paper, or on a computer disk, so that you can file it for future reference.)

PERSONAL CONFLICT SURVEY

Date completed: _____

a. How much conflict do you have to face in your own life? How many slaps, and how hard? If you had to estimate this on a scale from 1 (almost no conflict at all) to 10 (very frequent—perhaps almost constant—disagreements and experiences of hostility), what number would you choose?

b. Where do most of the conflicts in your life happen? In your personal life, your work life, your social life, your church life, or in some other area? Draw a pie graph—a "conflict pie"—and divide it into "slices" that show this information. Maybe you need only tiny slices for your social life and work life, and all the rest of the pie goes to your personal life.

c. Draw another pie graph. This time, divide it to show roughly how much of the conflict in your life goes with each of the *roles* you fill. Do you encounter most hostility when you're filling the role of parent? boss? student? daughter? Something else?

d. Who are the "predators" in your language environment? Make a list of them and of when and where you're most likely to have to deal with their hostility.

e. Is there a specific situation (or a set of situations) in which you know in advance that conflict will happen? For example: "When my teenage son comes in late at night, after his curfew, there's no **way** we can talk without a fight!" Make a list.

f. What kind of verbal conflict do you dread the most? What kind do you find most hurtful?

g. Are there situations in your life in which you know that you yourself are handing out the verbal slaps? What are they?

h. How do you honestly feel about verbal conflict? Look at the statements below; does one or more of them express your personal opinion on the subject?

- "Sticks and stones will break my bones, but words will never hurt me. As long as conflict stays verbal, it's not important."
- "I'd much rather have someone hit me than say cruel things to me; when you get hit, it's over right away, but you never get over the horrible things people say."
- "Only wimps worry about arguments—it's only words."
- "Verbal slaps are just part of the way the game is played. There's nothing wrong with them."
- "Arguments and verbal sparring aren't serious, they're a lot of fun! Normal people **like** to argue!"

- "Verbal slaps are necessary to keep things running properly in this world; most people won't do what they are supposed to do unless you use **some** kind of force."
- "I admire people who can really cut others down to size with words; it's a valuable skill."
- "Verbal force is completely different from physical force. There's no connection between the two things."
- None of the above. "My personal opinion is. . . ."

i. What is the worst verbal slap that you remember, from your entire life? Who gave it to you, and what was your response? If you could do it over again, would you change anything?

j. What is the worst verbal slap that you remember giving someone else, from your entire life? Whom did you give it to, and what was the response? If you could do it over again, would you change anything?

k. On a scale from zero (never) to ten (always), how often does verbal conflict in your life escalate to physical conflict? Is this a problem for you?

2. Set up a Conflict Journal for yourself, so that you can track your progress as you learn how to turn the other cheek in your own life. The most effective way to do this is to use either a big three-ring binder and ruled notebook paper or a computer disk, so that you have the greatest possible freedom as you work with the journal. You can file your Personal Conflict Survey there to serve as a baseline.

THOUGHT BITES

1. The word for gentleness in the New Testament is *praotes*. In *The Spirituality of Gentleness,* Judith C. Lechman says that "righteous anger" is *part* of gentleness and defines it as "the wisdom to understand our anger, the strength to harness it, and the restraint to act upon our angry feelings with self-control" (1987, 150). And then she says, "The righteous anger of *praotes* is a nonviolent weapon with which we can arm ourselves to do spiritual battle" (156).

This quotation is a good example of the semantic thickets that the Warrior metaphor can cause even the most careful person to stumble into. What would a "nonviolent weapon" be? If we "arm ourselves" with it to do spiritual battle, how can it be "nonviolent"?

2. "Ph.D. in Leadership, Short Course: Make a careful list of all things done to you that you abhorred. Don't do them to others, ever. Make another list of things done to you that you loved. Do them for others, always" (Dee Hock, in Waldrop, "Trillion-Dollar Vision," 1996, 79).

This has a nice ring to it, but would it work? To find out, try making the lists.

3. "I don't know why you're worrying so much about the inerrancy of Scripture . . . you're not going to do what it says anyway. If you're supposed to be a pacifist, if you're supposed to give your money to the poor—you're not going to do all this stuff" (Tony Campolo, quoted in Griffin, "Partying with God," 1991, 37).

4. Most Christian fiction today presents "an explicitly Christian worldview—a realm where prayer, conversion, and spiritual warfare are the normal realities" (Terrell, "Contemporary Christian Literature," 1996, 7).

5. "During the American Civil War, Abraham Lincoln made a speech in which he referred sympathetically to the southern rebels. An elderly lady, a staunch Unionist, upbraided him for speaking kindly of his enemies when he ought to be thinking of destroying them. His reply was classic: 'Why, madam, do I not destroy my enemies when I make them my friends?'" (Ury, "Getting Past No," 1991, 13).

6. "Love is not sentimental. It does not pretend that evil men do not exist. It offers a way to deal with them" (Ferguson, "Crux," 1980, 10).

7. "Jesus' words do not describe the strategy of weakness but the restrained wisdom of a person who is fully aware of what is happening and of how potentially dangerous are the results when unthinking anger responds to anger in a crisis. The strategy Jesus advocates will require tremendous skill and inner resources" (Palmer, *Enormous Exception*, 1986, 54).

8. "Christianity . . . does not turn the young male away from being a warrior, but it does teach him to model himself on Christ, and thus to become a new type of male in human history: the knight bound by a code of compassion, the gentleman" (Novak, "New View of Man," 1995, 4).

CHAPTER ONE

LEARNING TO LISTEN

Come now, and let us reason together.
Isaiah 1:18

Living the spiritual life would be a lot easier if we could somehow arrange to be held accountable only for *our own active deeds*. This would let us feel confident, using such excuses as "I was just doing my job" and "I was only following orders" and "I was only minding my own business." We know that option isn't available to us, however. Because we are morally responsible for at least two *other* kinds of human misbehavior: (1) refraining from doing good things ourselves, and (2) taking no action to interfere with *others'* wrongdoing. This very inconvenient spiritual fact stands like a huge boulder in our path.

SCENARIO ONE

Clay Johnson knew the conversation ahead of him was going to be unpleasant, but putting it off would only make matters worse; he had decided to get it over with. As soon as he and Donald Park were alone in the office during the lunch hour, he took a deep breath and spoke up.

"Don," he said, "I've got to talk to you. I wish I didn't, but you leave me no choice."

Don's eyebrows rose; he looked warily at his colleague. "What's wrong?" he asked.

"The first time I saw you take five dollars out of petty cash," Clay told him, "I didn't think anything of it. Anybody can have an emergency—I've had them myself. But you didn't put it back, Don. And I've seen you do the exact same thing again twice since then. That's called **stealing**, Don, and it's **wrong**; it has to stop."

The younger man sat down on the edge of Clay's desk and stared at him. "Oh, come **on!**" he protested. "I've taken what, fifteen bucks? Maybe twenty? I'll pay it back when I can, Clay—it's no big deal!"

"It's stealing," Clay said flatly. "If it was twenty cents instead of twenty dollars it would **still** be stealing, and if you don't cut it out I'll have to report it."

"You're **kid**ding!"

"No. I'm not kidding, I'm absolutely serious."

Don stood up then, his face flushed, his fists clenched, and turned on Clay fiercely. "You sanctimonious, spying, mean-spirited **hypocrite!**" he yelled, almost spitting out the ugly words. "You'd rat on me, when you know how much I need this job, over a measly **twenty dollars?**"

Clay's stomach was in a tight knot, and his head was pounding, but he knew he was right, and he wasn't going to back down. "Yes, I would," he said, "if you force me to. But if you'll put back the money you've taken, and do the right thing from now on, I won't say anything, and we can forget this ever happened."

"Listen, man," Don said urgently, "I don't **have** the twenty bucks! My back is really against the **wall** here! I'm flat broke, and Sue doesn't get paid for weeks! Come on ... what kind of rat **are** you, **any**way? Where's your famous Christian compassion **now**, man?"

That did it. That was the last straw, and Clay lost his temper.

"**You're** the **rat** around here, Don," he said harshly, "not me! In fact, you're worse than a rat, you're a **thief**. You have a lot of nerve calling **me** names, buddy!"

"Oh, **yeah**? How about a few **more**?" Don taunted him. "How about PRUDE? How about SPY? How about—"

"Don?" said a voice behind them. "Clay? What's going on here?" The two men had been so angry that they hadn't even heard the door open; the voice belonged to their boss, Charles Hanniver, owner of CH Insurance.

Clay's heart sank. Now the fat was really in the fire. He didn't want to report Don's stealing; he didn't want to lie; he didn't want to stand by and seem to back up whatever story *Don* might come up with to explain their argument to Charles. What was he doing to *do*?

For the ten thousandth time, he wondered: *Why does doing what's right so often seem to create worse problems than the ones I started out with?*

WHAT'S GOING ON HERE?

This is a typical example of good intentions gone wrong. Not because Clay is mistaken in his opposition to what Don is doing, and not because he should have pretended that he didn't know and didn't care—Clay is right about both of those things. But he has handled this very badly.

POINTS OF VIEW

Don is a young man just getting started in his career and married life, facing the usual problems that go with that set of circumstances. He knows it's wrong to take money out of petty cash, but it seems to him to be a very *trivial* kind of wrong, and he really does mean to pay the money back when he can. He sees it as borrowing—borrowing without permission, sure, but not **steal**ing. It was because he saw it as so minor that he didn't bother trying to hide what he was doing from Clay. It never entered his head that the older man, already well established and financially secure, would take such a hidebound position. He knows Clay is a Christian; the man isn't shy about his beliefs, and the two families go to the same church. But Christianity as Don understands it is supposed to mean being *good* to your neighbor, not turning him in to the boss for borrowing twenty measly bucks!

The way Clay sees it, however, when you sit back and let people do things that are immoral, without making any effort to stop the wrongdoing, you're just as guilty as they are. And Clay doesn't consider stealing, no matter how small the sum, a trivial matter. He's sorry that he lost his temper, but he never dreamed that the thief—caught in the act and being offered a fair chance to make things right—would turn on *him* and start making accusations.

The clue to this particular communication breakdown is in Clay's own words to Don: *"You leave me no choice."* Clay responds to his personal feeling that he's trapped by putting Don in a situation where *Don* has no choice. And he manages to do it so badly that in the end he himself faces still more bad choices: ruining Don's career by telling the truth, doing wrong himself by lying, or doing wrong by failing to point out someone else's lie. All he's managed to do is blunder from one moral quandary to another, with nothing to show for his efforts.

I can't give you an exact statistical percentage, but I can make a very confident guess: I am sure that at least half of all communication breakdowns (perhaps far more) happen *because people are unaware of their existing language choices*. That's what has happened here. The problem is: Clay feels obligated to transmit a message that has negative content, and he's unaware that *positive* ways to deliver such messages are available to him. He believes that hostile language is his only choice for the task.

There are quite a few communication errors in the scenario; we'll go over them when we take another look at it. Right now, however, let's concentrate on just one section, where a single major and very common error—*failure to listen*—is demonstrated. Look at this pair of utterances carefully; they are important to understanding what went wrong, and why. And then keep them in mind while we turn to a discussion of the listening process.

Don: Oh, come **on**! I've taken what, fifteen bucks? Maybe twenty? I'll pay it back when I can, Clay— it's no big deal!

Clay: It's stealing. If it was twenty cents instead of twenty dollars it would **still** be stealing, and if you don't cut it out I'll have to report it.

A COMMUNICATION TECHNIQUE: TRUE LISTENING

Psychologist George Miller once said something so critically important to good communication that I've always called it "Miller's Law." He said:

In order to understand what another person is saying, you must assume that it is true and try to imagine what it could be true of. (Hall, "Giving Away Psychology," 1980, 46)

That is, when someone tells you "My toaster is talking to me!" the proper response isn't "Oh, don't be ridiculous! **Toas**ters don't talk!", but "What is your toaster saying?" Not because you *accept* the claim that a toaster can talk, but because you are willing to *assume*—however briefly—that it's true, while you listen carefully to what comes next so that you can find out what the claim might be true *of*. There are quite a few possibilities. It might be true of the world experienced by someone suffering from schizophrenia; it might be true of someone whose toaster is making strange noises that could be interpreted as cries for help or warnings of imminent collapse. But the listener will never know either of those things if the response is "Oh, don't be ridiculous!"

Unfortunately, this is how most of us react when we hear something that strikes us the wrong way. "Don't be ridiculous!" (and Clay's response to Don) illustrates what I see happening everywhere I go: the practice of using not Miller's Law but something we could call "Miller's-Law-in-Reverse." It would go like this:

> In order to *mis*understand what another person is saying, decide that it's false. Then try to imagine what's wrong with the person who *said* it that would account for the unacceptable speech.

This is one reason why the "turn the other cheek" commandment is so hard to deal with. Your natural inclination is of course to apply Miller's-Law-in-Reverse, because the message seems so outrageous. But you can't do it—because the "person who said it" is God, and there can't be anything wrong with God; God is *perfect*. Since you can't blame this Speaker, you decide, by default, that something must be wrong with YOU.

Now let's look one more time at the lines of dialogue between Clay and Don:

Don: Oh, come **on**! I've taken what, fifteen bucks? Maybe twenty? I'll pay it back when I can, Clay—it's no big deal!"

Clay: It's stealing. If it was twenty cents instead of twenty dol-

lars it would **still** be stealing, and if you don't cut it out
I'll have to report it.

Don has said something that strikes Clay as outrageous and
unacceptable: that taking the twenty dollars is trivial, "no big
deal." Clay immediately decides that that's false and concludes
that the *reason* Don said it is that he has no morals and thinks
stealing is just fine. This is Miller's-Law-in-Reverse in action.
Almost always, as in the scenario, it will guarantee communication breakdown.

Suppose Clay had instead assumed that "it's no big deal" was
true, long enough to try to determine what it could be true of.
He can only do that by suspending his judgment about the other
man's character and listening carefully. *Just hearing what's said,
with a closed mind, won't do it.* Using Miller's Law would mean
that Clay would really listen, making it possible for him to understand that Don's utterance could be true in the world as it is perceived by someone who (1) agrees that stealing is wrong, but (2)
doesn't feel that taking twenty dollars from petty cash with the
intention of paying it back meets the *definition* of stealing.

If Clay applied Miller's Law, he would still disagree with that
second proposition. He defines stealing differently, and far more
rigidly. But he would not conclude that Don is a person with no
morals, who believes it's okay to steal. That conclusion—which
was based on no evidence and a failure to listen—was false. It
illustrates the meaning of the phrase "leaping to a conclusion."

This would change the situation in the scenario significantly
and for the better. Because there is a big difference between
behavior that follows from *disagreeing* with another person's
moral or religious principles, and behavior that follows from a
conviction that the other person *has* no principles! With that very
different perspective, Clay might not have lost his temper, the

two men might not have become so distracted by anger that they made their argument public, and they might have been able to come to an agreement.

Without true listening, good communication becomes impossible. Without true listening, you can't even be sure whether or not verbal blows are happening, much less make rational decisions about how to respond. Let's take just a moment to discuss how listening works and what true listening is, so that you'll understand why that's so.

WHAT IS LISTENING AND HOW DOES IT WORK?

If you go out on the street and ask people to explain the process of listening to human speech, most will say something like this: First you hear the words and figure out what they mean and then you put them together to find out what the whole sentence means, and so on. That seems logical, but it's false; listening that way would make understanding *literally* impossible.

The speed with which human ears and minds recognize and process speech has to interact with the human short-term memory (also called *the working memory*), which can handle only about seven chunks of information at a time and only for about thirty seconds. If you had to recognize each word and determine its meaning, and then combine the words into phrases and sentences and larger chunks and figure out *their* meaning, you would never understand more than the first sentence or two in any sequence of connected speech. You would fall far behind the speaker very quickly. Listening that way is impossible, in exactly the same way that running sixty miles an hour is impossible.

When you listen to speech coming at you, you immediately begin generating a stream of speech in your mind that represents what you believe will be said. (This doesn't mean that you are consciously aware that you're doing that; ordinarily, you aren't.)

You base this on your knowledge of the grammar of your language, your knowledge of the speaker and the situation, and similar factors. *Only when your highly educated "guesses" don't match what you hear do you stop and actually check out every word.* If you have good reason to believe Bill has just returned from Miami and he says, "Let me tell you about my trip to Chicago," that will stop you in your tracks. You'll say, "Wait a minute! Where did you say you went?" That's because when you heard "Let me tell . . ." you immediately generated a sequence meaning roughly "Let me tell you about my trip to Miami," and then, when Bill said "Chicago," you knew a correction was needed.

This listening process, like walking, is something you can do almost automatically; you don't have to know which hair cell in your ear or neuron in your brain to fire up. However, your mind can't come up with two different sequences of language at the same time. If, while people are talking to you, you're thinking about what you'll have for dinner, true listening is impossible. You can generate sequences of language that match the ones you're hearing *or* you can generate sequences like "I should have gotten more ground beef; two pounds isn't going to be enough. And I wonder if we have any potatoes? I'll bet we don't!" (Or a sequence such as "What Don just said is false, and he said it because he has no morals and thinks stealing is okay.") You *cannot* generate both sequences simultaneously.

This means that true listening (sometimes called "attending") is an active process, not a passive one. It's something you *do*, not something that happens to you. When you hear something that strikes you as unacceptable and respond with instant rejection followed by sequences like "He's only saying that to irritate me" or "She's saying that because she doesn't like me" or "He's saying that because he has no morals," all listening *stops*. When you instead use Miller's Law and give the speaker the benefit of the doubt while you go on paying attention to what's being said, listening happens—and understanding has a *chance* to happen.

You can always truly listen and then decide at the end that what was said really *was* unacceptable or outrageous. But that decision should be made on the basis of the information you get from listening, not by leaping to conclusions.

It's still true that a house built upon the sands cannot stand—there has to be a foundation. True listening is the foundation of linguistic understanding, and no other communication technique will help until that foundation has been established. Before you can use any of the other information in this book, you have to begin truly listening. Nowhere in the Bible does it say, "Come, let us reason separately"; it says "Let us reason *together*."

It may be that true listening is something you find difficult. It may even seem impossible. I know that many people who come to me for help claim that they don't have time to listen or that they just can't *make* themselves listen. Sometimes they say that nobody ever says anything to them that's worth the trouble of listening. (I have to wonder how, without listening, they can know that.) Don't be alarmed if this is a problem you share; you'll find help in the Workout Section for this chapter. Listening is a skill that you are fully equipped to learn, I promise you.

Now, let's go back and reconsider Scenario One in the light of the new information we now have.

ANOTHER LOOK AT SCENARIO ONE

Let's assume first and foremost that both Clay and Don are willing to truly listen to one another and apply Miller's Law as they talk. Even if no other deliberate change is made, that would help tremendously. But we can make a few other changes as well, while we're here, in response to strategic errors made throughout the scenario. Here are four of those errors.

First Strategic Error: Clay begins with this utterance: "Don, I've got to talk to you. I wish I didn't, but you leave me no choice." Don understands immediately that this signals trouble; he asks, "What's wrong?" Clay's utterance sets up a negative expectation before he has a chance to say another word, and it strongly implies that Clay has his mind made up before the "reasoning together" even begins.

Second Strategic Error: Clay tells Don that he's seen him pilfering the petty cash, which makes sense. But then, without giving Don an opportunity to say anything at all, he says "That's called **stealing**, and it's **wrong**. It has to stop." However convinced Clay may be that what he saw was stealing, it's a communication error to make the judgment and announce the verdict without giving the presumed wrongdoer an opportunity to explain.

Third Strategic Error: When Don tries to tell Clay that he doesn't really consider his actions stealing, Clay doesn't listen. Based entirely on his preconceptions, Clay delivers a brief sermon followed by an ultimatum: "It's stealing. If it was twenty cents instead of twenty dollars, it would **still** be stealing, and if you don't cut it out I'll have to report it."

Fourth Strategic Error: When Don becomes angry as a result of the first three errors, Clay most definitely doesn't turn the other cheek! He gives Don back anger for anger, evil for evil, and joins him in a contest of name-calling and insults. In the process, he throws away all hope of achieving his original goal, which was to persuade the younger man to repay the twenty dollars and change his ways.

Each of the men perceives the other as having slapped him across the face, verbally; neither one is able or willing to turn the other cheek. It doesn't have to be like that; but neither man has to be cowardly or cringing, either. Both of these bad outcomes can be avoided. To see how, let's rewrite the dialogue in the scenario now, from the beginning, with two goals: applying Miller's Law as we go, and avoiding those four strategic errors.

Scenario One, Revised

"Don," Clay said, "I'd like to talk to you about something, if you have a minute."

"Sure," Don answered. "What's up?"

"I've seen something recently that worries me," Clay told him.

"Oh, yeah? What's the problem?"

"Several times in the past month I've seen you take money out of petty cash, and I've never seen you put it back. I'm more than willing to believe that I've misunderstood what I've seen; I'm more than willing to listen to your explanation."

There was silence in the room for a minute, and then Don spoke hesitantly.

"Okay, I know I shouldn't be taking the petty cash," he said. "But Clay, I've borrowed fifteen, maybe twenty, dollars. It's no big deal!"

"Borrowed it? You mean you've arranged that with the boss?"

"No," said Don, staring at the floor. "I mean that I'm going to put it back just as soon as Sue and I get paid. It's not like I was **stealing** the money!"

Clay sighed. "Don," he said, "I'm afraid you and I disagree on what stealing is. To me, if you take something without the owner's permission, that **is** stealing. Even if you mean to put it back. But I'm ready to hear you explain the difference to me."

Don cleared his throat. "I guess you're right," he said slowly. "Maybe. I just didn't think of it that way. So . . . what happens now?"

"How long is it till payday?"

"Three weeks for Sue, a couple of weeks for me."

"Okay. Let me make a suggestion. Here's your part: You put back five dollars a week until you've paid back twenty, and you don't take any more money for personal use without approval from the boss. Here's my part: I don't say another word about this, to you or anybody else. And here's **our** part: We put this behind us and go on as if it hadn't happened. How does that strike you?"

"It's fair," Don said. "It won't be easy, because I'm flat broke, but it's fair."

The two men could have negotiated this differently. They could have agreed that Don would pay *all* the money back at the end of the month. They could have agreed that he had to pay it back, on either schedule, and that the next time he found himself in a serious financial bind he'd ask Clay for help. Don could have stuck to his guns and insisted that taking small sums of money temporarily is borrowing rather than stealing—agreeing to *dis*agree about that—while still agreeing to pay the money back and take no more. Whatever the final outcome, their interaction would then have been a discussion and a negotiation, an example of reasoning together, instead of an undignified brawl.

Don and Clay are still the same two men in this revision, with the same ideas and principles and personal problems; they no doubt still disagree on many things. The message Clay wanted to deliver didn't change, and its content is no less negative. *The people, the facts, and the message are the same; only the language used to deliver it is different.* But the outcome of the interaction, with all its implications for their future relationship as colleagues and friends, has been moved from negative to positive, with no sacrifice of moral principle and without the loss of dignity and the verbal slapping around that took place in the original scenario. And Clay's communication goal—to persuade Don to change his behavior—now has a chance to be achieved. The relationship the two men have at the end of the revised scenario will allow them to go *on* reasoning together; this is the first step.

WORKOUT SECTION

1. Set up a page for your Conflict Journal like the one below, so that you can record the data and track your progress.

Miller's Law Incident Log

Date and Time:

Situation: *(Who was present, where you were, what was going on, and so on—just briefly.)*

What was said to me:

What I said back, using Miller's Law:

What was said next: [repeat as many times as necessary]

How it turned out:

What I learned from this incident:

---

2. Carl Rogers had more opportunity to listen to others than most of us do; it was part of his professional task to listen very carefully for long periods of time. He noticed that you can tell a lot about *how* people listen by observing what they say in response, and he identified a set of five listening styles that can be recognized by the utterances that are typical of them. Here's the set, with example responses (the first example in each case is positive and the second, negative).

a. Evaluative Listening:
- "That's a kind thing to say."
- "That's a stupid thing to say."

b. Interpretive Listening:
- "You're only talking like that because you're so tired."
- "You're only talking like that because you want to make me feel guilty."

c. Emotional Listening:
- "I'm sorry to hear about your problems—my heart aches for you. I just wish I could help you somehow."
- "It makes me feel **terrible** to hear you talk about your problems! I wish you'd just keep it to yourself!"

d. Probing Listening
- "Maybe it's not really as bad as you think. What were the **exact** words your boss said to you?"
- "Either give me the **exact** words your boss said to you or don't bother me about it at all!"

e. Summarizing Listening:
- "It seems to me that you've decided that your plan is impossible. Am I understanding you properly?"
- "What you mean is, you've made such a mess of everything that there's no way you can **fix** it now! That's what you're really **say**ing!"

In the same way that it's helpful to know the addresses and phone numbers of people you frequently interact with, it's helpful to know their typical language behavior. In Chapters 3 and 4 we'll take up the question of how to *deal* with these listening styles. So that you'll have the information you need then, begin observing your family and associates—and yourself—to identify the most frequent listening styles. Record the data in your Conflict Journal for later use. It's also important for you to answer these questions about yourself:

- What is *your* most typical listening style?
- Can you tell whether you usually answer with positive examples of a style or negative ones? Do you see any pattern?
- Do you rely on one listening style with some people and a different one with others?
- Can you identify any listening style as the one you're most likely to rely on in a disagreement?
- Do you feel that you have clear *reasons* for your listening style choices? (For example, "I respond like that because it's good manners" or "I never respond like that because I was taught **not** to when I was a child.")

3. If you need to improve your listening skills, your best learning strategy is to work with your television set. It's available at your complete convenience, and it can't get its feelings hurt. Tune in a program or play a videotape on which someone is talking at length (preaching a sermon, making a speech, giving a lecture, offering a lengthy explanation or narrative) and sit down and *listen*. Don't take notes—just listen. It doesn't matter if the speaker bores you; the more bored you are, the greater the challenge, and the more you'll learn. Every time you notice that your attention has wandered away from the speaker, grab it, drag it back, and start listening again. Set a timer for five minutes at the beginning of each session, and keep practicing until you can listen for the entire time without once letting your attention drift off to other things. When you've learned to listen deliberately and actively for five minutes, you're ready to start listening to human beings in the flesh. (If a lot of your listening has to be done on the telephone, practice with the radio or with audiotapes in exactly the same way.)

Go on with the rest of this book while you're working on your listening skills, by the way. Many of the things you'll learn in later chapters will help you listen better and more easily. Don't be surprised if at first you find that you can't keep your attention on the speaker for very long; I've had clients who at first found it impossible to listen even for thirty uninterrupted seconds. It may take you a bit longer to reach the five-minute goal, but you'll be able to do it.

4. Every utterance contains *two* messages—the one that you think of as its content, and another that is called the *metamessage* because it is a message *about* the other content. Parts of the metamessage may be in the words; but you'll remember from the Introduction that for English it's more often carried by body language, including tone of voice and the like. Being aware of the metamessages when you listen to others—and getting them right— is one of the most important skills you can have for preventing and resolving conflict. You don't want to imagine metamessages that aren't there; you don't want to miss the ones that *are* there; and you don't want to be unaware of your *own* metamessages.

If this is difficult for you, your TV set can once again help you. Tune in a program or video that shows people interacting with one another in a way that is reasonably like real-life conversation—not a game show or a sports program. Watch for a few minutes to become familiar with the characters and situation, and then *watch with the sound turned almost completely off, so that you can't understand any of the words being said.* Try to figure out the speakers' metamessages from their facial expressions, posture, movements, and tone of voice. Every so often, turn up the sound and check to find out how well you're doing.

When you first try this, you may need to look for just the most *basic* metamessages, such as "I'm angry" or "I'm afraid"; when you can do that easily, move on to "I'm angry with the cat"

17

and "I'm afraid of that tall man." Being absolutely correct every time isn't nearly as important as learning to pay attention to speakers in this way so that it will become a habit. However, if you're way off target—for example, you thought the metamessage was "I'm very angry," but when you turned up the sound you discovered that it had to have been "I'm very happy"—don't try to move to more detail until that improves. This sort of mismatch will happen once in a while because you *do* understand the metamessage; an actor may be saying happy things while really feeling angry and doing a rotten job of acting! But if it happens all or almost all the time, blaming it on an epidemic of bad actors isn't wise; it's probably you. Note: If you're not a native speaker of the language you're watching, this will be much harder for you than for native speakers. Not impossible, but harder.

5. My clients sometimes include people who flatly say that they can't be bothered learning to listen, because there's nothing in it for *them*. I'm always happy to be able to tell them that they're wrong, and that it has been proved that true listening is actually good for your health. To find out about this amazing benefit, I recommend reading the work of James J. Lynch. For example, read his book called *Language of the Heart: The Body's Response to Human Dialogue*, published by Basic Books in 1985.

Thought Bites

1. "Respect for the dignity of the other person created in the image of God requires that we not silence or exclude him but try to persuade him" (Neuhaus, "We Can Get Along," 1996, 31).

2. "[A] Christian can understand what a liberal atheist is saying, and can even imagine what the world would be like if what the atheist says were true, without believing a word of it" (Neuhaus, "We Can Get Along," 1996, 29).

3. In "Deep Listening," (O'Reilly 1994, 17), Mary Rose O'Reilly says that when you truly listen, with your full attention, "you begin to hear not only what people are saying but what they are trying to say."

4. "An essential part of true listening is the discipline of bracketing, the temporary giving up or setting aside of one's own prejudices . . . so as to experience as far as possible the speaker's world from the inside, stepping inside his or her shoes" (Peck, *Road Less Traveled,* 1978, 127).

CHAPTER TWO

SPEAKING THE SAME LANGUAGE

> He who refuses correction goes astray.
> **Proverbs 10:17**

When people haven't asked us for our advice, but we feel that it's our duty to offer it anyway, we know that what we say may not be welcome. We can well imagine that we might feel negative, too, if we were in the other person's shoes. Rejection hurts less in a case like that, because we're prepared for it and can understand it; turning the other cheek to such hostility may be relatively easy to do.

But when someone has come to us and *asked* for our help, rejection can be an unpleasant, and sometimes painful, surprise.

SCENARIO TWO

Hannah looked at the tearful woman sitting across from her and was sorry about the tears; at the same time, she was relieved, because maybe now she could *help*. Melanie Jones was someone people went out of their way to avoid. When a meeting or a choir practice could be scheduled without Melanie's knowledge, that was done. When a way could be found to leave her out of social events, that was done too. Everybody felt bad about it, but what choice was there? When Melanie was around, you couldn't get anything *done*! And now here she was at Hannah's kitchen table, in tears, offering Hannah the chance to improve matters by saying what nobody had dared to say up until now.

"Hannah," she wept, "I can't **take** it any longer! People don't want me around, and I don't know **why.** They knock themselves out to get **away** from me. And I just don't **get** it! I try so hard! **Why** is everybody so against me??"

"Listen, Melanie," Hannah said, trying to sound as compassionate as she felt, "I'm so glad you asked me, because the problem is really simple! No matter what's happening, you talk endlessly about your personal problems—that's all it is. People don't want to **hear** all that whining about every tiny detail of your life! It's depressing, and so much of it sounds so trivial. I promise you, dear: Talk about what **other** people talk about, instead of just talking about yourself and your own troubles, and everything will be different."

The silence went on and on; Melanie sat there staring at Hannah without making a sound.

"Did you hear what I said?" Hannah asked her uneasily. "Do you understand what I'm saying?"

"Oh, **I** understand all right!" came the answer, and Hannah flinched, shocked at the fury in the other woman's voice. "Sure, **I** get it! The 'problem,' as you put it, is that I fell for all that church garbage about caring for one another and helping each other out and making a community together! I really made a **fool** of myself, **did**n't I?"

"Melanie, please! That's not what I—"

"Don't you go 'please' at ME, Hannah Archer! You can stop preTENDing now! And you're wasting your whole Good Christian Lady act, too! I will never, NEVer, forgive you for this!"

Hannah was flabbergasted. She'd known that what she had to say might upset Melanie, and she'd been prepared to be patient and kind and talk it through with her, but this reaction stunned her.

"Melanie," she said slowly, "I can't believe my ears—you can't mean what you're saying. You **asked** me to tell you what the problem was! Remember?"

Melanie shoved her chair back and stood up; both hands on her hips, she answered through clenched teeth. "I came here and asked you to give me some **help**, Hannah Archer!" she said fiercely. "I didn't come here to have you tear me to PIECes! I hope you're SATisfied!"

Hannah would always be ashamed of the things she said during the fight that followed. But Melanie's words and attitude made her so angry, she lost every bit of self-control. It wasn't just that she didn't think about what to say; she didn't think at *all*.

What's Going on Here?

Here we have another of the classic communication breakdowns. A well-meant attempt to help—*help openly asked for and openly offered*—is met not with gratitude but with rage, and the entire interaction escalates from minor disagreement to full combat. It's bad enough when the person rejecting the advice is a child or a teenager; when it's an adult, as in this scenario, the gulf cut by an argument like this can be very deep and hard to bridge. And the perceptions these two women have of what *happened* could not be more different.

POINTS OF VIEW

As Hannah sees it, Melanie came to her and asked for help, and help was freely and compassionately given—and it was repaid with a vicious and inexcusable attack. This, to Hannah's mind, is worse than "an eye for an eye." Her perception of the incident is that she did *nothing* to deserve Melanie's abuse and that Melanie returned evil for good.

Melanie, on the other hand, feels that Hannah made a fool of her and that her sincere request for help was used as an excuse to cause her pain. After hearing Hannah's answer to her question, she feels that she can no longer hold up her head in her circle of friends and associates. How could she face them and talk to them, now that she knows what they think? She feels shamed and abused; she feels that she opened her heart to Hannah, something that is a sign of trust, only to be taken advantage of because she had made herself vulnerable. She finds the whole thing unforgivable.

An experience like this one can make the most compassionate and caring person feel justified in responding to others' troubles with a polite, "Sorry, I don't want to get involved." After all, if the result of loving thy neighbor is that the neighbor *attacks* you, why do it?

Many things went wrong in this scenario. It will be obvious to you that although Melanie started out listening to Hannah, her reaction to what she heard was a flagrant example of Miller's-Law-in-Reverse. She instantly decided that it was false and that Hannah had said it for the worst of motives, and all hope for communication ended right there. This was a serious error, enough in itself to turn a conversation into a pitched battle.

But there was something else going on in this interaction, something that is important for us to look at carefully: *There is a sense in which Melanie and Hannah weren't even speaking "the same language."*

A COMMUNICATION TECHNIQUE: USING THE SENSORY MODES

Human beings have to deal with a vast flood of information from their external and internal environments. From all the countless perceptions that pour over us, we have to choose the ones that we will notice and process. We have to decide which ones must be remembered and take steps to transfer them to our long-term memories with indexes that will let us bring them back to our consciousness when we need them again. We have to respond to all these stimuli in an astonishing variety of ways. We do this using our sensory systems: sight, hearing, touch, taste, smell, and a number of less familiar ones such as *proprioception* (the sense that lets us know where we are in space and helps us keep our balance).

By the time we're about five years old, we have discovered that one of our sensory systems—usually sight, hearing, or touch—is more useful to us than any of the others. That system is our preferred, dominant one; when we use it, we understand better, remember better, learn more, and are better able to accomplish our tasks in the world. Ask any kindergarten teacher about the ways that children learn. You'll get answers like these:

- "It's no use trying to just **tell** Johnny about things; he has to see a picture or a chart, or watch a film, or he just doesn't do his best work."
- "Ann can look at pictures and diagrams all day long, and she won't learn a thing—you have to **tell** her what she needs to know."

- "Tommy is one of those kids who just has to get in there with both hands and learn **hands-on**, or he's hopelessly lost. Looking at information or listening to it doesn't work for him at all."

Our sensory preference is also expressed in our spiritual lives. For some of us a feeling of closeness to God comes most easily from visual things, from looking at wondrous landscapes, seeing the ocean or the sunrise, or seeing the face of someone we treasure. For others it's the world of sound—hearing a symphony or a great choir, listening to a beloved hymn, hearing a sacred text read aloud, or hearing a loved one speak. (I'm hearing dominant myself, and when I hear the cry of a newborn child I feel the same bliss I find in listening to Gregorian chant.) Those who value touch above the other senses will feel most deeply moved toward the holy when they are held by a beloved person, or when they feel rain and wind on their face, or as their bodies are moving through space and time in dance or running.

Knowing a person's sensory preference is important to communication, because one of the ways it shows itself is in our *language* choices, especially when we are tense or upset. This is information we can put to excellent use. Under stress, we tend to rely heavily on the vocabulary—called a *sensory mode*—of our dominant sensory system, and to have trouble communicating in other sensory modes. The more tense we are, the more this happens, and the more problems it causes. In a severe crisis, the result of a mismatch in sensory modes can be very much like what happens to communication when someone speaks Navajo to a person who understands only French. The scope and scale are different, but the principle is the same.

Suppose that your boss has called you into his office and told you about a new plan he has for the business, asking you for your honest opinion. That's a stressful situation, even if you have only positive reactions to what you hear. The strain you feel will usually show up in your response.

- *If you're sight dominant:* "I see exactly what you mean—it's perfectly clear! It looks to me as if it would work really well—let's do it."
- *If you're hearing dominant:* "I like the way that sounds; it really rings a bell with me! It sounds like an excellent idea—let's do it."
- *If you're touch dominant:* "You've put your finger right on the heart of the problem; I get exactly what you mean! I feel like it would work really well—let's do it."

If we had only pleasant interactions with other people, this wouldn't cause communication problems. When we're at ease we use the vocabularies of *all* the sensory systems, moving from one to the other without the slightest difficulty. But life isn't like that. A great deal of the time, far more often than we would choose, we are involved in interactions that are anything *but* pleasant. We have to deliver bad news; we have to offer criticism and evaluation; we have to explain flaws and mistakes; we have to provide discipline and guidance; we have to refuse requests or make requests that we know will be unwelcome. Negative messages are part of human life, and we find ourselves involved with them on both the sending and receiving end of communication. And that is when knowing about the sensory modes and putting that knowledge to use can head off potential conflicts as well as defuse those that are already underway.

Notice the vocabulary choices that Hannah and Melanie—both tense, both wary—make in these lines from Scenario Two.

Melanie: "I can't **take** it any longer! People don't want me
around, and I don't know **why**. They knock themselves out to get **away** from me. And I just don't **get**
it! I try so hard. **Why** is everybody so against me?"

She can't *take* it. People don't want her *around*, and they *knock
themselves out* to *get away from* her. She doesn't *get* it. She tries
hard. Everybody is *against* her. All those items come from the
vocabulary of touch.

Hannah: "Listen, I'm so glad you asked me, because the problem is really simple. No matter what's happening,
you talk endlessly about your personal problems. . . .
People don't want to **hear** all that whining. . . . so
much of it sounds so trivial. I promise you, dear: Talk
about what **other** people talk about, instead of just
talking about yourself and your own troubles, and
everything will be different."

Hannah is hearing dominant. Her vocabulary choices, over
and over again, are *ask* and *talk* and *hear*; she talks about *whining* and things that *sound trivial*. And when her words are met
with silence, she asks, "Did you hear what I said? Do you understand what I'm saying?"

If Hannah spoke only Chinese and Melanie only Spanish, they
would both be prepared to have a terrible time getting even the
most basic messages across to one another. But because they
both speak English, it doesn't occur to them that "not speaking
the same language" could apply to *them*. They go right on speaking to one another in different sensory modes, and as their communication grows more hostile, they become more and more
tense—which locks them even more tightly into their own

dominant mode. This makes what was already a very bad situation worse. Fortunately, this particular problem can be easily fixed.

The rules for using the sensory modes are simple. You will recognize the mode you're hearing, automatically, because all the words and phrases of English are catalogued and cross-indexed in your internal mental grammar, and one of the ways they're indexed is by sensory system. When someone says "point of view" (or "a good grasp of the situation" or "music to my ears") you don't have to run to a dictionary to find out which sensory system is involved—you know, and you know instantly. You just have to be aware that this is something you should pay *attention* to. Once you've recognized the sensory mode in which the other person is speaking, here are the rules:

***Rule One*:**
Match the mode coming at you if you can.
***Rule Two*:**
Otherwise, try not to use any sensory language at all.

That's not hard to do. It is in fact so easy that people often assume it can't mean much. They say, "Nothing that simple could possibly work!" I assure you, using sensory modes with care *does* work, often in a way that seems almost miraculous. I get letter after letter from people telling me that there's someone they have always thought was just "a difficult person," someone they couldn't get along with no matter how hard they tried—until they learned about the sensory modes and tried matching that person's dominant mode. "It was like magic!" they tell me. "Suddenly, it was like he [or she] was an entirely different person!"

Matching someone's sensory modes can't work miracles, of course. And when people are relaxed and talking casually it's not even worthwhile. But a great many verbal battles happen because one or more of the people involved becomes too upset and distracted to think clearly. Anything you can do in a tense situation to *reduce* the stress in that language environment will help. It will help everyone present to avoid handing out verbal slaps themselves; it will help them resist the temptation to slap back when verbal slaps are aimed at them; it will help them reason together instead of doing battle. And it will make everyone more able to listen and more able to think before speaking.

Rule One—match the mode you hear—is the best choice. It makes the other person think, *Here's someone who can perceive the world the way I do; even if we don't agree, we can work together.* Rule Two—use no sensory language—is not as good, but it's much better than talking Chinese to the other person's Swahili. Answering "How bad does it look?" with "I don't see it as serious" is best. Answering it with "I don't think it's serious," using Rule Two, is not as good; but it's much better than answering with "I don't feel like it's serious," which is touch mode talking to sight mode.

Please don't underestimate the potential benefits of making this seemingly minor change in your language behavior. I know the first change I recommended to you, learning to truly listen, was a much larger change and required far more effort on your part. By comparison, using the sensory modes properly is *easy*. Be glad of that. It's a reason to rejoice. So many things are so difficult; we should be grateful that some genuinely useful and valuable things are simple. This is one of those things.

What if Hannah, the woman Melanie turned to for help, had known about using the sensory modes? What if she had recognized Melanie's touch dominance and had spoken to her in touch language instead of in her own dominant hearing mode? How might the scenario have turned out, with that change?

Let's go back to it and find out.

ANOTHER LOOK
AT SCENARIO TWO

The situation in this revision is unchanged, but the language (except for Melanie's opening plea for help, which clearly demonstrates her touch dominance to Hannah) will be very different.

Melanie: "I can't **take** it any longer! People don't want me around, and I don't know **why**. They knock themselves out to get **away** from me. And I just don't **get** it! I try so hard! **Why** is everybody so against me?"

Hannah: "I'd feel miserable too, in your place, and I'd like to help. But I feel like my answer to your question might really hurt you. You'll have to make up your mind whether this is something you really do want to know, painful or not. I'll need your word on that."

Melanie: [Stares at Hannah.] "You act like you're getting ready to say something **hor**rible!"

Hannah: [Shakes her head.] "No, I just need to be sure you grasp the fact that my message is serious, and that you may feel **bad** about it."

Melanie: [Swallows hard.] "Okay. I guess I'm braced for it, whatever it is! Go ahead."

Hannah: "The problem, Melanie, is that no matter what's happening **around** you, you go on and on about your personal problems. Melanie, people don't feel comfortable knowing every tiniest detail of your life, and they don't know what to say **back**. I don't think you're in touch with what's going on inside them through all this; it probably never enters your head that it rubs everybody the wrong way. But making the relationship you have with all of us smoother will have to mean that you carry more of your own load and join the rest of us in the things we're doing **together**."

[Silence. Melanie stares down at the table.]

Hannah: "Melanie, I'd like to know what you're feeling."

Melanie: [Voice shaking.] "Hannah—that really **hurt**!"

Hannah: "I know. I don't know how I could have put it in a way that wouldn't have hurt. But it wasn't done to hurt you—the point was to **help** you."

Melanie: "How about all that church stuff about caring for each other and loving your neighbor?"

Hannah: "One of the ways to do that, Melanie, is by not laying your burdens on your neighbors' shoulders except when you **truly** can't carry them by yourself."

Melanie: [Wiping away tears.] "I hate this. I **hate** it! But I really needed to know what I was doing **wrong**. Now that I know, maybe I can **do** something about it!"

Hannah: "I know you can; I'm counting on you."

Notice that Hannah's basic message to Melanie has not changed. It's still: *People can't enjoy being in your company if you complain constantly about every smallest detail of your personal problems.* Nobody wants to hear a critical judgment like that about themselves, and it's not easy to take. But Hannah has given it a shape carefully tailored to the touch vocabulary that Melanie is most at ease with under stress. This makes Melanie less tense and helps her find the strength and detachment she has to have if she is to understand the message and come to terms with it. She's still not happy, but she's not angry with Hannah, and she doesn't leap to false conclusions about the motives behind the message. Her final words give us reason to believe that she may be able to accept the information and use it to make things better in her life. This is a tremendous improvement.

Notice also that Hannah has taken the essential strategic step of warning Melanie that something difficult is coming, before she actually says it, and asking for specific permission to go ahead. She has also been careful to keep her speech free of sarcasm and hostility. And notice that she has dropped the remark about Melanie's concerns often seeming trivial to other people. That item of information isn't crucial to what she needs to tell Melanie, and it would add yet another layer of hurtfulness to the message. There's never an excuse for causing *unnecessary* pain.

THE SPECIAL PROBLEM OF TOUCH DOMINANCE

Before we leave the subject of the sensory modes, I need to explain one more thing to you. The trouble Melanie has communicating with Hannah in the original scenario is made worse by the fact that the two women have different sensory system preferences, yes. But it's important to understand that it's *worse* for Melanie than it would be if the two mismatched sensory modes were hearing and *sight*, because our culture is so strongly biased *against* touch.

We wouldn't send our children to school wearing blindfolds or earplugs; we wouldn't expect them to learn while obeying incessant commands of "Don't look!" and "Nice people don't listen!" and "Keep your eyes [or ears] to yourself!" We *do* insist, however, that our touch dominant children try to function in a "Don't touch! Keep your hands to yourself!" environment. For the child whose need for tactile information is just as strong as other children's need for eye or ear data, this is like having to wear heavy wool mittens at all times. The result is that these children tend to fall behind, to find themselves accused of "not trying hard enough," and to feel that they're always out of step and out of favor. As might be expected, this doesn't help them grow up to be pleasant people who are skilled at getting along with others. Often they are labeled "a flaming pain in the neck" as adults, even by family and friends; Melanie is a typical example.

We have to remember that some people in our society perceive every uninvited touch as either potentially violent or potentially erotic. They consider much touch language crude and vulgar, and they seem convinced that everything to do with touch—with the possible exception of the "contact" sports like football—is just plain *evil*.

This book is not an appropriate forum for a debate on this subject, but there are a few basic facts that we need to keep in mind. Suppose we set aside the issue of whether a strongly negative attitude toward touch is justified. It remains clear that where such an attitude exists it can cause very distorted perceptions of touch and that those distorted perceptions can lead to conflict. I have two recommendations:

1. When you interact with someone that you perceive as "a difficult person" or "a pain in the neck," pay close attention to that individual's language—it may be that he or she is touch dominant.
2. When you've recognized someone as touch dominant, make a real effort to speak with him or her in touch language— or, if you just can't bring yourself to talk "that way"—avoid sensory language as much as you can, in order to avoid a *clash* of sensory vocabularies. Then pay attention to what happens.

If you follow these recommendations, you may be amazed at how your perception of the person changes; a great deal of the time, the difficulty is not in the person but in the language.

A final note of caution: Remember that all of us, when we are relaxed and at ease, use all of the sensory vocabularies. Hearing someone use a few items from one sensory mode doesn't mean that it's their dominant mode. You recognize sensory dominance from language data when you observe that someone relies very heavily on a particular sensory mode in stressful situations. Here, for example, is a typical interaction between a touch dominant child and a sight dominant adult:

Child: "I can't do it! It's too hard! I just don't **get** it!"

Adult: "Don't be ridiculous! You're just not trying."

Child: "Yes, I **am** trying! I just don't **get** it!"

Adult: "Stop saying you don't 'get' it, for heaven's sakes! If you'd **look** at it, you'd understand it! It's right there on the **page**, you know, it's not written on the **ceiling**!"

Child: [Sullenly.] "I don't get it. I **don't**!"

Adult: "Now **see here**, young man! You . . ."

Both child and adult will grow more and more upset, which means they will grow more tightly locked into their own dominant sensory modes. The child will perceive the adult as mean and unfair; the adult will perceive the child as lazy and stubborn; verbal (and perhaps physical) conflict may well occur; and neither learning nor communication is likely to take place. And the child's preferences will not be changed by the constant struggle; like handedness, sensory dominance is a lifelong characteristic. If the child in the dialogue is fortunate, he may do well in spite of his problems and grow up to be someone like Tom Watson of IBM Corporation [quoted in "Adventures (and misadventures) of Watson Fellows," by Ted Gup, *Smithsonian Magazine* for 9/94, pp. 69–80, on page 78], who says: "I was a terrible student. I couldn't take that stuff off of the page and get it into my head."

You may find Watson's words crude and be surprised that someone of his stature would talk "that way" for the public press. That's exactly the point. That reaction is the problem, and it is a source of continual communication breakdowns—and many "turn the other cheek" encounters—in our society today.

WORKOUT SECTION

You can identify other people's dominant sensory modes by observing them over time and by carefully observing their language when they are communicating under stress. Determining your *own* sensory dominance, however—certainly something you need to know about yourself!—is often more difficult. It's hard to observe your own behavior and language objectively and accurately. The questions that follow will help you get started. (You may find that none of the answers offered is *exactly* what you'd say or do. That's all right. Just choose the one that comes closest.)

SENSORY MODES
PREFERENCE TEST

1. You've listened carefully as someone tried to persuade you to accept an idea with which you strongly disagree, and now it's your turn to talk. Which would you say?

a. "That's not the way I see it."
b. "That doesn't sound right to me."
c. "I don't feel like that's right."

2. You've just heard someone give an account of a problem that you're both facing, and you're amazed at how different it is from the way you'd present it. Which would you say?

    a. "Look, I don't think you're seeing this problem clearly at all."

    b. "Listen, what I'm hearing from you just doesn't represent the facts of the problem."

    c. "I don't get it—I don't think you have a very good grasp of this problem."

3. Your friend is feeling depressed about a project that you're sure will turn out all right eventually; you want to help. Which would you say?

    a. "You'll look back on all this one day and wonder how you could have seen it so negatively."

    b. "One day you'll remember the things you were saying today, and you won't believe you could have sounded so negative."

    c. "Down the road, you're going to feel completely different about all this; it'll get better."

4. You're giving a talk, and suddenly someone challenges you from the audience. Which would you say?

    a. "I always welcome other points of view."

    b. "I'm always willing to listen to other ideas."

    c. "I'll always be ready to make room for other ideas."

5. You and your spouse have had a serious argument, and you'd like to put matters right, but you're not willing to back down. Which would you say?

    a. "Please, can't you try to see things my way, just this once?"

b. "Please, couldn't you try to speak my language, just this once?"

c. "Please, won't you go along with my feelings, just this once?"

6. You've been selected to decide how a new U.S. coin will be decorated on one side. Which would you choose?

a. A picture of a favorite plant or animal

b. Your favorite brief saying

c. A deeply carved border around the edge of the coin

7. Your doctor has ordered you to take up a hobby for the sake of your health. Which would you choose?

a. Pencil sketching

b. Singing in a choir

c. Making pottery

8. In a restaurant, which of the following things would be most likely to make you leave without finishing your meal?

a. A whole fish on someone's plate, head and all

b. A song you hate, being played over and over

c. A miserably uncomfortable chair

9. You have to write a short article for a church newsletter. Which of these topics would you choose?

a. "How Our Church's Future Looks to Me"

b. "The Story of Three Favorite Hymns"

c. "Carving out a Role in Our Church Today"

10. You can afford to make a handsome gift to your local college. Which would you choose?

a. An original oil painting in a beautiful frame
b. A piano for the student union
c. A marble sculpture for the front lawn

All A answers are typical of sight dominance, B answers favor hearing, and C answers favor touch. Count your totals; six or more from a single category is evidence that it may be your dominant sensory system.

1. One of the perennial problems touch dominant people face in our culture is a shortage of *reading* material that uses lots of touch language. It turns up in technical manuals for fixing cars and doing surgery and wiring buildings, but not everyone is interested in such things. It's also found in books with explicit sex and violence; I'm convinced that a need for touch language may explain the otherwise puzzling popularity of those two kinds of writing. And there are a few writers of quality work—Annie Dillard, for example, and surgeon Richard Seltzer—who are unquestionably touch dominant and whose work reflects that fact. But some of the most powerful touch language is to be found in the Bible itself, and not just in accounts of battles or the Song of Solomon. For example: "How long will you torment my soul,/And break me in pieces with words?" (Job 19:2) and "He who gives a right answer kisses the lips" (Prov. 24:26).

If you're someone who finds touch language offensive, it would be a good idea for you to search for more examples like these two and give them some careful thought.

2. For your Conflict Journal, set up a page like the one below and begin keeping track of Sensory Mode Incidents. As with all "log" pages, repeat the "what was said to me/what I said back/what was said next" lines as often as is necessary.

Sensory Mode Incidents Log
Date and Time:

Situation:

What was said to me in _____ mode:

What I said back:

What was said next:

How it turned out:

What I learned from this incident:

When an encounter went badly and ended in conflict or confusion, consider how you might have used the sensory modes technique to turn it around. Rewriting the incident as we rewrote Scenario Two is good practice for the next time.

3. In the same way that it's useful to know the listening mode preferences of people you frequently interact with, it's useful to know their sensory mode preferences. Hearing them suddenly shift into that mode will be a clue that lets you know they are feeling tense or upset. When you know in *advance* that something will upset them, you can anticipate the need to use their dominant sensory mode and be prepared. I'd recommend adding that information to your records, including your telephone index.

4. Another good item for your Conflict Journal is a collection of very good examples, spoken or written, from each of the three major sensory modes. It's especially useful to collect examples from the mode that's last on your own preference list, because that's the one you would find hardest to match in a language interaction. And it's good practice to try to "translate" the examples in one mode into the other two, just to find out where and how difficulties are likely to arise.

5. Go back to your personal conflict survey and take another look at the situations where conflict is most likely to occur in your life. There are probably half a dozen lines that you hear over and over in such situations. Write versions of each one in all three major sensory modes. For example, suppose that one of your common "hot button" situations is in your job at a clinic, where you are forever hearing this line: "Your doctors charge **way** too much for an office visit!" You could then write this set of possible responses:

- "Patients don't always have a clear picture of the costs of health care today, Mrs. Smith."
- "Health care charges that sound high are often based on factors that patients don't understand, Mrs. Smith."
- "Patients sometimes feel that medical charges are high because they're not really in touch with the reasons behind them, Mrs. Smith."

THOUGHT BITES

1. "We persuade others by speaking their language" (Cunningham, *Faithful Persuasion,* 1990, 46).

2. "For I know it as given that God is all good. And I take it also as given that whatever he touches has meaning" (Dillard, *Holy the Firm,* 46).

3. "Is there—even if Christ holds the tip of things fast and stretches eternity clear to the dim souls of men—is there no link at the base of things, some kernel of air deep in the matrix of matter from which the universe furls like a ribbon twined into time?" (Dillard, *Holy the Firm,* 47).

This (like #2) comes from Annie Dillard's book called **Holy the Firm;** even the title of which uses touch language. Could you "translate" it into sight or hearing mode? Notice how the task of trying to translate, whether you find it doable or not, helps you more deeply investigate this difficult quotation.

CHAPTER THREE

AVOIDING VERBAL CONFLICT AT WORK

A soft answer turns away wrath,
But a harsh word stirs up anger.

Proverbs 15:1

People sometimes complain that a spiritual life is made even more difficult by hard-to-understand parts of the Bible, and they're quite right. But the Bible's position on human quarreling is in *no* way obscure! Over and over again, the book of Proverbs warns us against strife, contentiousness, and perverse language. It's better, we're told, to live in a corner of a housetop than in a house that's shared with a contentious woman; quarrelsome men are given equally sharp rebukes. The Almighty, we're informed, hates people who sow discord.

The New Testament is equally specific. Not once does it say, "Blessed are those who argue so skillfully that whenever they're in a fight, they always win." It says, unambiguously, "Blessed are the peacemakers." It's all perfectly clear.

What tends *not* to be clear is that the Bible does not forbid anger itself, nor the expression of anger. Being angry when that anger is righteous and justified is allowed, and we're expected to speak up about it. The four things that we're told to avoid are anger that is quick and thoughtless, anger over trivia, anger as a *first* resort, and the unjustifiably harsh expression of anger of any kind. This creates two problems for human beings:

1. How can we tell the difference between acceptable and unacceptable anger?
2. When we *must* express anger, how can we do it gently, without violence?

As we begin exploring those two questions in this chapter, we'll see once again that the difficulty is far more often in people's language than in their characters and morals. As David S. Cunningham tells us in *Faithful Persuasion*: "If we are to distinguish the blessings from the cursings, the good from the evil, we must pay extraordinarily close attention to our language" (1990, 29).

SCENARIO THREE

Cecily Blandon's job as checkout clerk at the hospital had its pleasant moments, but this wasn't going to be one of them; she knew the minute she saw Charles Hanniver heading her way that she was in for trouble. His wife wasn't doing well; her heart condition was too serious to make a quick and easy recovery possible. She handed him the bill he asked her for and braced herself for what was coming—and he didn't disappoint her.

"This is unbe**liev**able!" he said sharply. "Just **look** at this total—it looks like the state budget for a **year**! You can't seriously expect me to **pay** this!"

"I'd be glad to explain the figures, sir," Cecily said carefully, trying to keep a neutral expression on her face. "I'm sorry you think they're too high, but—"

"They're not just **high**, Miss Blandon, they're **outrage**ous! How can you have the **gall** to hand me this when my wife is lying in this hospital suffering, right this **min**ute? Don't you have any human feelings at ALL?"

That really stung. Cecily was so tenderhearted, she couldn't even watch *Lassie* reruns without crying; how *dare* this man accuse her of having no human feelings! She stared right through him and answered him in an icy voice.

"You **asked** me for your bill, Mr. Hanniver," she said. "It wasn't **my** idea to give it to you now, it was **yours**! And I only **work** here at Vendon Memorial, I do **not** set the **rates**!"

"And you don't CARE about them EITHer, DO you, Miss Blandon?" he answered, nearly shouting at her now. "As long as you get your paycheck, you couldn't care LESS what happens to the helpless people who have to deal with this place! We're just a bunch of NUMbers to YOU!"

"You are NOT just a bunch of numbers!" Cecily shot back, her voice shaking with outrage. "NOTHing is more important to this hospital than the PAtients and their FAMilies!"

"Oh, YEAH? Well, you have a funny way of SHOWING it!"

"MISter Hanniver—" Cecily began. That was as far as she got. The voice that interrupted her came from her supervisor, and it wasn't friendly.

"What seems to be the **prob**lem, Cecily?"

WHAT'S GOING ON HERE?

This is communication breakdown taking place in public, and the people involved have plenty of things to blame their anger on.

POINTS OF VIEW

Charles Hanniver is frantic about his wife. He loves Maria; seeing her sick and in pain is tearing him apart. He knows the hospital has to charge for its services, but that's just *intellectual* knowledge; his *heart* keeps insisting that asking someone for money when help is so desperately needed is simply wicked and cruel. All day he's been trying to get Maria's doctors to tell him what's going to happen to her; all day he's been told only that the doctors are very busy and will get back to him when they can. He hasn't dared make a scene about it, for fear that they'll refuse to talk to him at all. And now—looking at the sum of money the hospital is charging him, which strikes him as charging him to be ignored and abused—he's just out of control. He's too exhausted and too overwrought to remember that the woman he's shouting at has no responsibility for any of his problems.

Cecily Blandon isn't a child, and she understands that people in crisis often lose control and say things they don't really mean. After the incident was over, she was ashamed of having lost her *own* self-control, because she knew she didn't have that excuse. But at the time, the things Mr. Hanniver was saying and the way he was saying them struck her as so unfair and vicious and deliberately hurtful that she couldn't think straight. In the heat of the moment, with him yelling at her in front of everybody, both her training and her common sense failed her. And, she thinks: *No matter how upset he was, he had no **right** to talk to me that way! I couldn't just stand there like a doormat and let him walk all **over** me!* She's sorry it happened, and sorry to be in trouble with her supervisor; but it really seems to her that she didn't have much choice.

Cecily is mistaken. She had a set of very clear choices, all of them stored in her internal grammar with a set of equally clear rules for selecting among them. Unfortunately, this wasn't knowledge she was consciously aware of, and so she was unable to make deliberate use of it.

We learn our native languages in infancy, without any formal instruction. We learn them in a way that we never learn chemistry or geography, creating a store of what is called *internalized* knowledge. That's a good thing in many ways, but it also causes problems. The information we need about using our language is in there ... somewhere ... but we have no idea how to get at it! It's like owning a huge library that has no card catalogue or other indexing system: Finding what you need is mostly a matter of blind luck. In the next section we're going to bring some of that information out into the light of day and attach indexes to it, so that from now on you can use it freely and systematically.

A Communication Technique: Using the Satir Modes, Part One

The most important thing to understand about the interaction in Scenario Three is this one fact: *Cecily does know, at some level, that her own anger is unjustified and therefore unacceptable.* She does know that Mr. Hanniver's behavior is nothing more than a demonstration of his despair and fear, and that the real target of his verbal slaps is not her but the universe at large and the American medical system in particular. Nevertheless, she doesn't *think* of that at the time. Instead, she loses her temper and becomes part of a degrading public brawl! *Why?* There are two reasons, one linguistic and one neurological.

The linguistic reason is that Cecily felt forced to defend herself against a verbal attack and brought into play all her internalized rules for hitting back with language. Using our culture's Warrior metaphor, she accepted the rule that says the only available roles are Winner, Loser, and Fleeing Coward; like any good Warrior, she was determined to be the Winner. But that reason won't suffice, because she knew the attack wasn't really directed at her and was caused by panic rather than an intent to harm. The reason that matters here is the *neurological* one.

Human beings once had to be ready to flee or fight on literally an instant's notice. In the days when we routinely faced wild animals in our daily lives, there was no time to stop and carefully consider whether we were in danger. We had to respond instantly and ask questions later. Once in a very great while, we *still* have to do that, and for that purpose, a part of the brain—the *amygdala*—is always on sentry duty. Messages coming in from your environment do go to the reasoning part of your brain, to be considered with as much care as may turn out to be necessary. But the amygdala, sitting there scanning for danger, can go off like a smoke alarm in a fire, causing you to react *before* you have a chance to think it over.

This has nothing to do with your character or your moral fiber or your faith. Daniel Goleman, in *Emotional Intelligence,* accurately calls it an "emotional hijacking." A portion of the information headed for your rational cortex is grabbed by the amygdala with a "THIS COULD HURT ME!" response, and you react as you would react to a rattlesnake. Later, when your rational mind has pointed out to you that there *wasn't* any rattlesnake, you will think, "How in the world did **that** happen?? I don't know what came **over** me!" But then it's too late.

There *will* be times in your life when you will truly need to be able to call on the strength of your faith and resolve. Times when you will truly need to be able to resist temptation if you are to follow the command to return good for evil. There will be times when someone *will* revile you and spitefully use you and say all manner of evil against you falsely. The reserves of moral strength you need in such crises are precious, and limited; they should be saved for *those* situations, not wasted in every trivial disagreement that comes along! The situation that Cecily found herself in in the scenario was *not* a situation of that kind.

You can't turn off your amygdala any more than you can turn off your lungs or your ears, but you *can* do something about its wild alarm response. To do this, you'll have to bring to conscious awareness some decisions that you're used to making by habit or almost at random, something you're well equipped to do. A major step toward that goal is to learn to recognize the set of language behavior patterns called *Satir Modes* and to make choices among them consciously and deliberately, just as you have learned to do with the sensory modes. All this information is in your internal grammar already, I promise you; you just need to be put in touch with it in a way that gives you ready access to what you know.

RECOGNIZING THE SATIR MODES

Dr. Virginia Satir was a world-renowned family therapist. Over the course of a lifetime of practice, she noticed that people who were communicating under stress tended to use one of five language behavior patterns. She named them Blaming, Placating, Computing, Distracting, and Leveling. We'll go through that set and examine the patterns; you'll find them very familiar.

Let's imagine that five people, each with a different preferred Satir Mode, are in an elevator together—and suddenly, with a screech, the elevator stops between floors. In that situation, *everyone* is under stress! Our five people would then say things like these:

The Blamer:
"WHY do things like this ALways happen to ME? Did ONE OF you turkeys push the wrong button, or WHAT?"

The Placater:

"Gosh, I HOPE I didn't push anything I wasn't supposed to! I mean I COULD have—YOU know me, I'm SO clumsy!—but I don't THINK I did! If I did, I'm SO SORry!"

The Computer:

"Elevators get stuck between floors once in a while; it happens. Someone will fix it any minute now."

The Distracter:

"We're STUCK, and we're gonna be here for HOURS! That's what ALways happens, don't you KNOW THAT? I mean, not that I'M any expert on elevators—I could be WRONG! You KNOW? Sometimes things do get fixed. But this is the LAST time I get in any stupid ELevator, I can TELL you THAT!"

The Leveler:

"I'm scared."

The characteristics that identify these patterns are already stored in your internal grammar for your use—that's why you find them so familiar. Here's the list that will let you set up indexes for the stored information:

Blaming: Lots of personal language; lots of extra emphasis on words and parts of words; heavy use of words such as *always* and *never* and *everybody* and *nothing,* as if no exceptions exist; a surface impression of anger and hostility. And hostile body language to back it all up, such as scowls and clenched fists and *looming* over people.

Placating: Lots of personal language; lots of extra emphasis on words and parts of words; a surface impression of apology and a desire to please others at all costs. And the body language of (as Satir put it) a cocker spaniel puppy.

Computing: As little personal language as possible, with many generalizations and abstractions and hypothetical items; no emphasis on words and parts of words except what absolutely cannot be avoided; a surface impression of neutrality and control. And the minimum of body language—very little movement or facial expression, very neutral intonation and tone of voice.

Distracting: A rapid cycling through all the *other* Satir Modes, switching from one to the other seemingly at random, with body language changing each time to match the mode. A surface impression of total panic and confusion.

Leveling: None of the above. That is, communication under stress, when it has none of the characteristics of the other Satir Modes, is Leveling. Leveling is the simple uncontaminated truth—so far as the speaker knows—truly spoken.

I want to add one word of caution here. When I describe these patterns in seminars, someone always says something like, "Oh, yeah! My Uncle **Will** is a Blamer!" That's understandable, but it's not accurate. Nobody "is" a Blamer or any of the other labels. As with the sensory modes, people tend to have a preferred Satir Mode and tend to rely on it heavily whenever they're tense or upset. But *unlike* the sensory modes, that preference shifts and changes with the situation.

What most people do is rely on one Satir Mode when under stress at work, another in tense situations at home, perhaps still another somewhere else. The preferences are linked to the roles they happen to be playing. It's very common for people to Placate with doctors ("Doctor, PLEASE, I just KNOW there's SOMEthing you can DO!") and Blame with nurses ("Nurse, WHY don't you DO something??!"). We don't know whether the sensory mode preferences are something you're born with, something you learn, or both; we do know that the Satir Modes are behavior that is *learned*, usually as children observe the language behavior and communication strategies of adults and older youngsters around them.

When we refer to "the Blamer," then, it's just shorthand for "the person who, at this moment, is using the language behavior pattern called Blaming." And the same thing is true for the other Satir Modes.

Because these patterns are stored in your internal grammar, and because you now have them labeled and indexed, you will automatically recognize the Satir Mode coming at you. The question is, then, how do you respond? Which Satir Mode do you choose? It should *be* a deliberate choice, not a choice based on habit, not a mindless amygdala-inspired reaction to supposed danger. With the sensory modes, your choice was easy: You match the mode coming at you if you can. Choosing among the Satir Modes is based on the same principles, but it's a little more complicated.

RESPONDING TO THE SATIR MODES

Remember that human language encounters are *interactive feedback loops,* and that anything you feed is sure to grow. Here are the loops that can be predicted if you match a Satir Mode:

Blaming back at Blaming guarantees a fight:
    X: "WHERE did you put my BOOK?"
    Y: "LISTEN, it's YOUR book! YOU find it!"
    X: "Hey, YOU HID it—now YOU FIND it!"

Placating back at Placating will get you an undignified delay:
    X: "Where shall we go for **lunch**?"
    Y: "Where do **you** want to go?"

X: "You know me, wherever **you** want to go is **fine** with **me**! YOU pick!"

Y: "No, I wouldn't THINK of it! YOU decide!"

Computing back at Computing creates a dignified delay:

X: "There's undoubtedly a solution to this problem."

Y: "When the solution is known, something can be done."

X: "Finding the solution is the first step."

Y: "Solutions are sometimes hard to find, however."

Distracting back at Distracting is panic feeding panic; we all know what that would be like, without examples.

Leveling back at Leveling is the simple truth, as the two speakers understand it, going both ways:

X: "I'm scared."

Y: "Me, too."

And also:

X: "You don't like me, do you?"

Y: "No. I can't stand you."

An exchange of the simple truth is theoretically perfect communication, but it won't necessarily be made up entirely of positive messages.

When you look at this information and remember how feedback works, you'll be prepared for the first Satir Mode rule: You've recognized the mode coming at you, and you ask yourself, "Do I want this to grow?" If so, you match that mode. If someone is Blaming at you, and a fight is what you *want*, Blame back; a Blaming loop always ends in a fight.

The other rule—the one you fall back on if matching modes would give you an outcome you object to—is also a matter of common sense. Computing is the most neutral of the Satir Modes and therefore the least likely to lead to problems. The second rule is: "If you don't know what to do, go to Computer Mode and stay there until you have a reason to do something else."

The Satir Modes technique is a complex subject in many ways; we're going to continue discussing it in Chapter 4 in much more detail. For now, however, based just on the information we have at this point, let's go back and see how it might be applied to the interaction between Cecily Blandon and Charles Hanniver.

ANOTHER LOOK
AT SCENARIO THREE

Suppose Cecily had been familiar with the use of the Satir Modes when she had her encounter with Charles Hanniver. Remember: She knew that he was in great distress and likely to be unreasonable; she braced herself for what was coming. She wasn't taken by surprise. What could she have done to head off the emotional hijacking and subsequent fight that nevertheless happened in the scenario, without sacrificing anyone's dignity? Let's rewrite the dialogue to reflect the change.

Mr. Hanniver: "This is unbe**liev**able! Just **look** at this total—it looks like the state budget for a **year**! You can't seriously expect me to **pay** this!"

Cecily: "I'd be glad to explain the figures, sir. I'm sorry you think they're too high, but—"

Hanniver: "They're not just **high**, Miss Blandon, they're **outrag**eous! How can you have the **gall** to hand me this when my wife is lying in this hospital suffering, right this **min**ute? Don't you

	have any human feelings at ALL?"
Cecily:	"People have a very hard time thinking about money when somebody they love is in pain."
Hanniver:	[Sighs.] "You're right; they do. And that's what's wrong with me right now. I know none of this is your fault; I'm sorry I took your head off like that."
Cecily:	"It can happen to anybody—no problem."
Hanniver:	"Do I have to think about this bill right now?"
Cecily:	"No, sir; we haven't even billed your insurance company yet. Just put it away for later."

Notice what happened here. Charles Hanniver came at Cecily Blandon in full and unrestrained Blamer Mode. Not because he had a quarrel with her and not because he thinks she's at fault, but because he's under more stress than he's able to handle. When Cecily fed that hostility loop in the original scenario by Blaming *back* at him, returning slap for slap, they had a terrible (and completely unnecessary) fight. Answering in *Computer* Mode as she does in the revision above prevents the escalation of hostility and heads off the fight before it even begins. Instead of a fight there is an apology, courteously accepted, and a return to rational communication.

Cecily's Computer Mode response—"People have a very hard time thinking about money when somebody they love is in pain"— is a flawless example of turning the other cheek. She has not hit back, and she hasn't done any groveling; she has simply demonstrated that she's not frightened and sees no need for combat. Her response is appropriate, dignified, and entirely free of hostility. Crucially, nothing about it could cause either her or Hanniver to lose face.

When Cecily offers that Computing response rather than hitting back, she is making a conscious choice instead of acting on the basis of habit or *re*acting without thinking. She doesn't have to be saintly; she doesn't have to call on the reserves of moral strength and courage which should be reserved for genuine emergencies. She just has to pay attention and recognize the Satir Mode she hears; she chooses her Satir Mode response on the basis of her linguistic knowledge and her knowledge of the circumstances. She is fully capable of doing this, and so are you.

Adults aren't frightened when a toddler comes running at them screaming in rage. They *know* this is no threat to them, and no alarm goes off in their heads. If they have responsibility for the child, they will make an effort to teach a lesson about manners and self-control, but the only emotion they will feel is amusement or mild annoyance. In exactly the same way, we can learn to recognize verbal slaps like those Charles Hanniver was handing out as no threat to us and react to them with compassion and gentleness—expressed in Computer or Leveler Mode—rather than with fear or anger.

In my work with hospitals over the past twenty years I've seen this scenario—both versions—take place many, many times. I've seen the same scenario (with slightly different scripts) in other kinds of businesses and public places; I've seen it in homes and schools and churches. And I have always been amazed at how quickly the anger can be defused! Certainly there are times when a single Computer Mode response to the Blaming isn't enough, and the person on the receiving end of the hostile language has to hang in there and return Computing for Blaming two or three times before the Blamer gives up the toxic behavior. That happens not because the Blamer is perverse but because the Blamer isn't listening; it can take a while for a message to get through the dense fog of intense distress and panic. But the strategy almost always works. When it doesn't, something else, something unusual, is going on. (For example, the verbal attacker could be mentally ill or under the influence of drugs.) And a great deal of the time it works as quickly as in the revision.

A FINAL NOTE ABOUT THE SATIR MODES

Human beings have three interacting channels for spoken communication: the words they say, the body language that goes with those words, and the channel that (having no formal name) is usually called "vibes," that in some mysterious way carries wordless and very broad messages about inner feelings. When all three channels match, that's called *congruent* or *syntonic* communication. With all the Satir Modes except Leveling, a mismatch exists between the obvious external message and what's really going on inside the person speaking. Understanding how this works is an important part of being able to turn the other cheek with a "Notice, friend, I'm not afraid of you at all!" message and *mean* it. Here are the basics:

Blaming:
- Outer message: "I have ALL the power! Look OUT!"
- Inner message: "I don't have any power. . . . If I don't throw my weight around, nobody will do anything I want."

Blaming ordinarily indicates that the person speaking feels insecure and is trying to hide that feeling behind hostile language.

Placating:
- Outer message: "I don't care."
- Inner message: "I CARE! I care so MUCH!"

Placating indicates that the speaker is afraid to make people angry. It's not that the speaker doesn't care, but that he or she cares so deeply and is worried about negative reactions.

Computing:
- Outer message: "I don't have any emotions."
- Inner message: "I have one or more emotions I don't want you to know about."

Computing shows the smallest amount of mismatch between outside and inside messages. Often there are excellent reasons not to reveal some inner feeling, and Computer Mode makes it possible to do that.

Distracting:
- Outer message: "I'll say EVERYthing! What I want to say might be IN there somewhere!"
- Inner message: "I don't know what to SAY! HELP!"

In all four cases, the speaker's words will say one thing, but the body language and the vibes will contradict the words to some degree. That's why Computing tries to keep body language to a minimum—so that it won't betray the mismatch. Only with Leveling can you be certain that the words and the body language match the speaker's inner feelings. The Leveler who says "I'm going to hit you" and raises a fist *is* going to hit you; the Blamer, using the same words, probably won't do anything more than threaten and bluster.

When I tell people about all this, they often start to be concerned about the morality of the Satir Modes. I understand that, and I respect the concern. After all, we're not supposed to lie— isn't it lying to feel one thing and deliberately say another?

We'll be coming back to this issue again. For now, I'd like you to postpone making a final decision about it and do three things for me.

First, remember the basic linguistic facts. Because whatever their ethical implications, they set out the actual language behavior of people in the real world, and they represent what you should expect to encounter as well as what you yourself do.

Second, consider the following situation. Suppose you know a child who is truly ugly—not just a bit short of the cultural ideal for beauty, but *really* ugly. When that child comes to you and says, "I'm really ugly, right?" is it your moral obligation to answer with "Yes, you are—you're a truly ugly child"? That would be telling the truth; it would be Leveling. But would it be loving your neighbor as yourself? And would it be doing to that child what you would want done to you?

Third, remember Cecily Blandon's response in Computer Mode to Charles Hanniver's hostile language. Her inner feelings were, "He has no right to talk to me that way; but he's only doing it because he's in such distress, poor man, that he can't think straight." She didn't express those feelings, however. She said only, "People have a very hard time thinking about money when someone they love is in pain." The question is: Was she bearing false witness in some way? Certainly the statement she actually *made* was entirely true. Think about it.

WORKOUT SECTION

1. As with the other language behavior characteristics we've discussed, it's useful to know the Satir Mode preferences of people with whom you frequently interact. Suppose you have to attend a meeting that you know is likely to become contentious. It's helpful to know that the person chairing the meeting usually relies on Blaming for stressful public communication and that the person who sits next to you can be expected to use Placating in such situations. Knowing that, you can plan ahead, and you won't be as likely to become involved in arguments by accident. When you have to discipline teenagers or criticize employees, knowing in advance that they will probably respond in a particular Satir Mode helps you prepare. I recommend adding Satir Mode preference information to the records in your Conflict Journal and to your telephone index.

2. You may be unaware of your own Satir Mode habits; in my experience, most people are. But this is something you need to know about yourself. It's not easy to find out; as you've discovered, being an objective and accurate observer of your own language behavior is difficult. There are two things you can do that will help you get the information you need. First, set up a Satir Mode Incidents Log page for your Conflict Journal like the Sensory Mode Incidents page (substituting "Satir" for "sensory"), and begin keeping records to serve as your database. Second, answer the questions that follow, choosing the answer that is *closest* to what you would actually say or do.

- Someone you love has just said to you, "YOU are the most EXTRAVAGANT person I ever KNEW! I've never before seen ANYbody throw money away like you do!" Assume that it's true that you aren't careful with money. Which of these things would you say back?
  a. "How I spend my money is MY business!"
  b. "I know . . . but PLEASE don't carry on about it like that! I'm SORry!"
  c. "Sometimes it's hard to understand another person's spending habits."
  d. "I've known several people who are as extravagant as I am."
  e. All of the above.

- You're supposed to be on a diet, and you've just gotten caught sneaking ice cream out of the refrigerator in the middle of the night. The family member who caught you says, casually and without any particular hostility, "I thought you were supposed to be on a diet." Which would you say back?
  a. "Just **keep** your thoughts to yourSELF, okay?"
  b. "Shoot . . . I NEVer DID have any will power!"
  c. "Lots of research indicates that diets don't work."
  d. "I hate it when I get caught cheating."
  e. All of the above.

- Your tax preparer has just told you that you're going to have to pay five hundred dollars more income tax than the original estimate, saying, "I'm sorry. I must have missed something." Which would you say back?
  a. "I don't PAY you to miss things, I pay you to get it RIGHT!"
  b. "DON'T tell me that, PLEASE! I thought I could TRUST you—you KNOW I did!"
  c. "Anybody can make a mistake."
  d. "I'm sorry to hear that—five hundred dollars is a lot of money."
  e. All of the above.

- You've taken your car in to be fixed, and you're in a hurry, but your mechanic says, "Sorry, I can't get to it today." Which would you say back?
  a. "What do you MEAN, you can't get to it today? I NEED it today!"
  b. "Oh, NO! You KNOW how busy I AM! YOU can fit it in someplace, I KNOW you can!"
  c. "No schedule is set in concrete; there's always a way

to make a few changes."
d. "If you don't get to it today, I'll be in real trouble."
e. All of the above.

- Someone has just turned on you and snapped, "YOU think you know EVERYthing, DON'T you?!" You're amazed; you have no idea what brought this on. Which would you say back?
  a. "What's the MATTER with you?"
  b. "Of COURSE I don't think that! WHY would you ASK me a question like that??"
  c. "Nobody knows everything."
  d. "That question doesn't make any sense. Want to tell me why you asked it?"
  e. All of the above.

- You've just been told that you failed an important exam. You knew you wouldn't get a high score, but you can't believe that you did *that* badly. Which would you say back?
  a. "WHAT? Is that supposed to be a JOKE?"
  b. "**Oh**, well . . . I don't care!"
  c. "It happens."
  d. "I don't think I did that badly. Are you sure?"
  e. All of the above.

- You're stuck in an elevator with a friend, who says, "I'll bet this **scares** you, **does**n't it?" Which would you say?
  a. "What do you MEAN? I don't scare THAT easy!"
  b. "Why do you say THAT? Why are you trying to make me FEEL bad, at a time like THIS?"
  c. "Everybody gets scared in a stuck elevator."
  d. "Yes, it does."
  e. All of the above.

- You've always sung an Easter solo at your church, but now your minister has called you in and said, "I'm sorry, this year somebody else will do the solo. I know you won't mind." You *do* mind. Which would you say back?
  - **a.** "If you know I won't MIND, why are you SORry?"
  - **b.** "[Sigh.] I guess my voice just isn't very GOOD any more . . ."
  - **c.** "Decisions like that are tricky—mistakes can easily be made."
  - **d.** "Sure I mind; I want to do it. Let's talk about it."
  - **e.** All of the above.

- You've just taken a short self-test to try to find out something about your own Satir Mode patterns. The person who wrote it asks you whether you think it was useful.
  - **a.** "How COULD it be? It's only nine questions LONG!"
  - **b.** "Oh, YOU'RE the expert on things like THAT! I don't know anything about TESTing!"
  - **c.** "An accurate Satir Mode preference test would probably have to be at least fifty questions long."
  - **d.** "It's not long enough, but it shows me what I need to be watching for."
  - **e.** All of the above.

The A answers are all Blaming, B answers are Placating, C answers are Computing, D answers are Leveling, and "all of the above" goes with Distracting. If you see no pattern in your answers—if you chose one or two of each—that may also indicate a tendency toward Distracter Mode.

3. If you feel that handling anger is especially difficult for you, I recommend reading Dr. Frank Minirth and Dr. Les Carter's book titled *The Anger Workbook.* It has lots of case histories, lots of helpful Bible quotations, and much wisdom.

4. If the *St. Elsewhere* television series is available to you in syndication, watch a few episodes and pay careful attention to the language behavior of heart surgeon Mark Craig. He is the closest thing I can imagine to being truly a Blamer; unlike real people, he uses Blaming for almost every purpose and in almost every situation. This is particularly ironic, since Craig's style of speaking has been proved to be a strong predictor of heart attacks.

THOUGHT BITES

1. "If I know somebody very well, in ten minutes, if I set my mind to it, I could perhaps say to them things so cruel, so destructive, that they would never forget them for the rest of their life. But could I In ten minutes say things so beautiful, so creative, that they would never forget them?" (Bishop Kallistos Ware in "Image and Likeness," 1985, 66).

I've spent a great deal of time thinking about this question since I first read the interview, and it continues to baffle me. I've tried, unsuccessfully, to construct messages "so beautiful, so creative" that the person I said them to would never forget them. Why should it be so easy to say something unforgettably wicked, and so hard to say something good that's equally unforgettable?

2. "Hate is the accumulation and sedimentation of anger unresolved, unconfessed, and denied over long periods of time" (Oates, *Psychology of Religion,* 1973, 313).

3. "To function successfully in our complex world it is necessary for us to possess the capacity not only to express our anger but also not to express it" (Peck, *Road Less Traveled,* 1978, 65).

4. "One reason that many otherwise 'good' people use words irresponsibly and cruelly is that they regard the injuries inflicted by words as intangible and therefore minimize the damage they can inflict. For generations, children taunted by playmates have been taught to respond, 'Sticks and stones can break my bones, but words (or names) can never hurt me.' But does anyone really think that a child exposed to such abuse believes it? . . . Words are powerful enough to lead to love, but they can also lead to hatred and terrible pain. We must be extremely careful how we use them" (Telushkin, "Words," 1996, 2).

CHAPTER FOUR

AVOIDING VERBAL CONFLICT AT HOME

**The beginning of strife is like releasing water;
Therefore stop contention before a quarrel
starts.**

Proverbs 17:14

In Chapter 3 we discussed the effective use of the Satir Modes as a way of avoiding conflict in a business environment. In this chapter we're going to expand on that discussion and consider how the same technique can—and should—be used between family members.

People sometimes tell me they don't feel they should have to worry about carrying on civil and courteous communication with their spouses and other members of their own household. They say things like this: "Come on, they're my **family**! **They** know I love them. They unde**rstand** me! I don't have to watch what I'm saying around **them**, for crying out loud!"

It's true that our families are likely to put up with us when others might not do so. We can usually count on them to make excuses for our hostile language in a way that others would refuse to do. And I agree that we ought to be able to let down our hair and be ourselves with our families; that's one of the things that makes family and home so dear to any human being. But there's one thing we must remember:

Verbal slaps hurt far more *when they come from someone we love.*

Even when we understand what provoked the hostile language, even when we realize that we were in some way at fault ourselves, it still hurts more than verbal abuse from people who don't matter to us.

Scenario Four

Joe Johnson's hands were white-knuckled on the steering wheel as he drove himself and Helena home from the lunch at the Country Club. He knew his face was grim and his jaw was tight; he just hoped that their friends hadn't noticed how upset he was.

"Helena," he said harshly, as soon as they were safely in their lane, "that crack you made about my memory was a **low blow**! 'When Joe gets up in the morning, he can't even remember his **name**!', you said. Can't even remember my NAME! How could you DO that to me?"

His wife turned to stare at him, frowning. "**Hon**estly, Joe!" she said. "Can't you take a little **joke**? It was **noth**ing!"

"It wasn't 'nothing' to ME, Helena!" he told her angrily. "YOU made me feel like an IDIOT back there—in front of EVERYbody! YOU have no consideration for me at ALL!"

"Now, WAIT a minute, Joe! That's—"

"I MEAN it!" he insisted, cutting her off. "You DON'T!"

"That's not FAIR! Who cooks your **meals**, who takes care of your **clothes**, who—"

"YOU don't do that for ME, Helena!" he said, furious now because she hadn't so much as said she was sorry. "You do all THOSE things for yourSELF, so you can brag about what a champion WIFE you are!"

There was a long silence. When she finally answered him, her voice was cold and distant. "Well, THAT'S easy to fix!" she said. "From now on you can just take care of yourSELF, Joe Johnson!"

Joe was flabbergasted. *She* humiliated him in front of all their friends, in public. *She* made a nasty crack about him for no reason at all. And now *she* was angry with *him*! It was unbelievable!

"BLAST it all, Helena!" he yelled, smacking the steering wheel with his fist. "WHY is it impossible to have a simple adult discussion with you? What's the MATTER with you, ANYway? Have you lost your MIND?"

She sat beside him rigidly now, with an expression on her face that she knew he hated, the one he called her "martyr look." "Well?" he insisted. "Well? Don't you have ANYTHING SENSIBLE TO SAY?"

"Joe," she answered slowly, staring out the window, "living with you is like LIVing in a COMbat zone."

"Oh, is that SO! Well, let me tell YOU something, Helena! If that's true, it's YOUR OWN FAULT—and you DESERVE it!"

WHAT'S GOING ON HERE?

Anything you feed will grow. Remember? Here we have two people who genuinely care about one another, who have lived together for decades, and who are busily feeding a hostility loop, with no regard for the damage it may do to them and to their relationship with one another. Turning the other cheek is obviously the *last* thing on their minds!

Joe made his opening complaint about Helena's behavior in Blamer Mode; Helena fed the hostility by Blaming back at him; Joe fed the loop again and raised the hostility level another notch by putting heavier emphasis on words and parts of words . . . and so it went, round and round the loop. By the time the dialogue between Joe and Helena is over (which will be long after they've arrived home), both of them will have said things they don't mean and will deeply regret later.

POINTS OF VIEW

Joe is nearing retirement age, and he's sensitive about it; he's especially worried because lately he's been having a little trouble remembering things. He's certain that Helena knows how he feels about this. The way he sees it, there are only two possible explanations for her behavior at the Country Club lunch. Either she didn't even consider the consequences of what she was saying, which shows a completely unacceptable level of thoughtlessness, or she deliberately humiliated him in front of their friends, using a line she knew would really hit him where he was most vulnerable. He knows it's not true that she only looks after him and their home to get compliments for herself, he knows she enjoys her role as homemaker and takes pride in it, and he knows she loves him. But that's exactly the *point*! How could she do such a thing to somebody she loves? And she didn't even *apologize*! It seems to Joe that the only way he could hold up his head after such a rotten trick was by hurting Helena back as badly as she hurt *him*. He had to make her understand that what she did was wrong, that he absolutely will not allow her to treat him that way, and that she must *never* do such a thing again.

And Helena? She was sorry the instant the words about Joe's memory problems left her mouth. She can't imagine what could have made her say what she said, except that she's worried about Joe, too, and it was on her mind. It just slipped out. She had intended to tell Joe how sorry she was, the minute they were alone. But he didn't give her a chance! He turned on her before she could say a word, and the things he said hurt her terribly. The way she sees it, she and Joe are even now—he's more than paid her back for her small slip of the tongue. And there's no *way* she's going to explain or apologize, not after the awful things he said to her! She knows why he lashed out at her, she knows she was in the wrong, and she knows he loves her as much as she loves him. But that's exactly the *point*: You don't talk to somebody you love the way Joe talked to her—ever! It seems to her that she had to hurt Joe back as badly as he hurt *her*, so he would know that what he did was wrong, that she absolutely will not allow him to treat her that way, and that he must *never* talk to her like that again.

Joe and Helena are both right and both to blame; this is an equal opportunity argument. Helena shouldn't have said what she said about his memory in the first place, neither in public nor at home; and she should have apologized to him for it and explained that it was an accidental slip of the tongue. Joe shouldn't have attacked Helena for the slip without giving her a chance to explain, and he shouldn't have reacted with such violence to a single, careless sentence spoken in front of friends.

Helena shouldn't have responded to his anger by counterattacking; Joe shouldn't have fed the flames by continuing to give her slap for slap. But the fight presented in this scenario is typical of what happens when wrong Satir Mode choices are made, even by two people who love and understand one another and in situations where there's much to be said on behalf of both sides.

The worst thing about this episode is that it's *entirely unnecessary*. Joe is justified in wanting to deliver his negative message: the complaint about Helena's remark. He's right to be outraged. But there were many ways he could have expressed his anger and achieved his communication goal without giving the negative content a negative *form*. In previous chapters we've looked at only one potential revision of the opening scenarios. It would be very unusual for only one such choice to be available to the speakers. This time, let's look at a number of different ways things could have been handled more satisfactorily for everyone involved.

Using the Satir Modes,
Part Two: Another Look at Scenario Four

In the original scenario, there are only two logical explanations for the Satir Mode choices. One is that Joe and Helena both deliberately chose Blaming in order to have as vicious a fight as possible. If that's what was going on, their problem is far beyond the scope of this book, and it's not a problem of language. The other explanation—the one we'll assume must be accurate—is that they both relied on whatever Satir Mode they habitually use for personal conflict, without making any deliberate choices at all. Suppose they don't do it that way. Suppose one or both are familiar with the Satir Modes technique and were willing to use it in this situation. How might things have gone?

Revision A

Joe: "Helena, that crack you made about my memory was **a low blow**! How could you DO that to me?" [Blaming]

Helena: "Nobody likes to have their problems turned into jokes, especially in public." [Computing]

Joe: "Right! Exactly. I wish you wouldn't do that again, Helena." [Leveling]

Helena: "I won't—you have my word. It was just a slip of the tongue, and I'm sorry." [Leveling]

Here, Joe opens with Blaming, which is a poor choice. But Helena responds with Computing, and Joe then drops his hostility and switches to Leveling. This sequence (the same one you saw in Scenario Three) is the most typical one for defusing a potential argument.

REVISION B

Joe: "Helena, that crack you made about my memory was a **low blow**! How could you DO that to me?" [Blaming]

Helena: "It was thoughtless of me, Joe, and I'm sorry." [Leveling]

Joe: "Do you think I'm overreacting?" [Leveling]

Helena: "No; I was wrong." [Leveling]

Joe: "Okay—we'll forget it ever happened. Fair enough?"

Helena: "Fair enough." [Leveling]

This time Helena responds by Leveling, and she and Joe quickly reach agreement on the issue. This couldn't have happened in Scenario Three, because the hospital clerk had done nothing to apologize for. Since Helena *is* in the wrong, however, her response is appropriate. If she had set it to a different tune—"It was THOUGHTless of me, Joe, and I'M so SORry!"—it would have been Placating, and a poor strategy; there are no good combinations of Placating and Blaming, because both are uniformly hostile language. But as a Leveling utterance, it's exactly right.

Notice that Helena does not—as she would in many popular television shows that serve as communication models for our youngsters—respond to Joe's suggestion that they forget it ever happened by saying "That should be **easy** for **you**! YOU can't remember anything ANYway!" A line like that isn't clever or funny, and it's unfortunate that such lines get heavy applause in our media. In a situation of conflict, they serve no purpose except to start a new fight.

REVISION C

Joe: "Helena, when you joked about my bad memory in front of everybody at lunch, it hurt. The way I keep forgetting things isn't funny to me—it worries me." [Leveling]

Helena: "I'm sorry, Joe. It worries me, too; I guess I just had it on my mind." [Leveling]

Joe: "I'd feel a lot better if you wouldn't do that again." [Leveling]

Helena: "I won't. You have my word." [Leveling]

Joe: "Thanks, honey." [Leveling]

In the first two revisions Joe makes his objections in Blamer Mode and Helena is careful not to Blame back, so that the hostility is defused and the fight doesn't happen. In the C revision, *Joe* is more careful. He delivers his negative message, but he does it in Leveler Mode, and Helena matches his choice.

None of these revisions requires Helena to grovel, but all three require her to acknowledge that she was wrong. Suppose Helena is one of those people who just can't bring herself to do that; what we learned about her from observing her behavior in the original scenario makes that a reasonable idea. Could the fight still be avoided, even if Joe isn't saintly? Let's try one more rewrite, and see.

REVISION D

Joe: "Helena, that crack you made about my memory was a low blow! How could you *do* that to me?" [Leveling]

Helena: "Nobody likes to have their problems turned into jokes—especially in public." [Computing]

Joe: "Right. Exactly! I wish you wouldn't do that again." [Leveling]

Helena: "One person's joke is another person's serious insult, but people who'd rather not live in a combat zone know it's a good idea to be careful about that kind of thing." [Computing]

Joe: "Absolutely. I knew you'd feel the same way about it that I do." [Leveling]

How do you feel about this fourth possibility?

When I present a dialogue like Revision D in seminars, people—of both genders—often object. They tell me that "Joe shouldn't have let Helena get **away** with it like that!" Helena was the one who was in the wrong; therefore she is supposed to be the one who "loses," they tell me.

People who've focused more on Helena's point of view, who feel that Joe overreacted and "made a mountain out of a molehill," also object—and they tell me that it was Helena who let *Joe* "get away with it" and should instead have stuck to her guns until *he* apologized! As they see it, Helena has been wronged, and it's Joe who is supposed to "lose."

I'm not going to be the Omniscient Writer here and rule on who is most in the wrong. *It doesn't matter.* And I must point out that both those rooting for Joe and those on Helena's side appear to have forgotten that there *is* a command to turn the other cheek. What does matter is being aware that both attitudes expressed above come straight out of the Warrior metaphor rule book, from the set of rules for Conversation As Combat. They have no place in a marriage, and they represent a serious misunderstanding of the linguistic facts.

Remember that both Joe and Helena really did understand one another. (That is one of the primary reasons why fights between people who care about each other are often so vicious: They know one another so well that they know *exactly* what will hurt the most.) If we were to write out Revision D as the emotional metamessages only, instead of surface messages, it would look something like this:

Joe: YOU HURT ME A LOT WHEN YOU MADE THAT CRACK ABOUT MY MEMORY, ESPECIALLY SINCE YOU DID IT IN PUBLIC.

Helena: I KNOW THAT ANYBODY WOULD BE HURT IN THAT SITUATION.

Joe: RIGHT. I DON'T WANT YOU TO EVER DO THAT AGAIN.

Helena: WE DON'T ALWAYS AGREE ABOUT EVERYTHING, BUT WE AGREE THAT WHAT I SAID *THIS* TIME WAS A MISTAKE AND SHOULDN'T HAPPEN AGAIN.

Joe: YES, WE DO; I KNOW THAT. AND I'M GLAD IT'S TRUE.

Suppose Joe is an expert tennis player and Helena isn't very good at tennis. We wouldn't call him a wimp when he cut her a little slack in their tennis games; we'd consider it a reasonable way for him to behave. We'd say it demonstrated both courtesy and common sense. Why, then, if Joe is more skilled at communication than Helena is, should we fault him for extending that

same behavior to their shared communication? It's far more important than tennis!

Joe's goal is to make it clear to Helena that he strongly objects
to what she did and wants her to refrain from such actions in the
future. *Revision D accomplishes that goal.* And Joe knows that
although Helena finds it impossible to *say* "I was wrong and I
regret it and I won't do it again," that is in fact what she *means.*
Similarly, Helena understands why Joe spoke to her so harshly
and knows that he will be sorry when he's had time to calm down;
insisting that he apologize would accomplish nothing useful and
tell her nothing she doesn't already know.

Joe would gain nothing by humiliating Helena with his greater
skill in a tennis match; if he insisted on doing that over and over
again, she'd refuse to play tennis with him anymore. Exactly the
same principles hold in communication. If either partner turns
every disagreement into a contest or combat and insists on fighting to win every time, pretty soon there won't *be* any communication. This is how people find themselves being asked for a
divorce "without any warning."

The four revisions are not examples of saintly forbearance.
They don't show Joe or Helena tapping the reserves of moral
strength they should be keeping for genuine emergencies.
They're simply examples of what happens when Satir Mode
choices are made with full awareness and for good reasons that
are consistent with the speaker's communication goals. You *are*
going to use the Satir Modes when you communicate under
stress, because they're part of the grammar of English. The
only way to avoid them is to live a life in which there *is* no tension or anxiety, an option unavailable to us in this world. Since
you have to use them, it's much better to make your choices
skillfully.

But What About St. Paul?

St. Paul said that in the same way Christ is head of the church, the husband is head of the house. Promise Keepers speaker Tony Evans has expressed that idea for today's men, advising them to announce to their wives that mistakes have been made, that the wives have been carrying too much of the leadership burden as a result, and that the men are now taking back the role God meant them to have.

One of Paul Watzlawick's clients told him about her experience in an argument with her husband, who, after she had convinced him she was correct, said, "Well, you may be right, but you're still wrong because you're arguing with *me!*" If I were to write about communication within the family without discussing this particular issue, touchy and difficult and politically charged though it may be, I would be hiding my head in the linguistic sand. The question is: Must a woman always agree with her husband as long as what he says isn't literally mad or evil, because that is her *spiritual* duty? And is it a man's moral obligation to *insist* that she do that?

I'm not a theologian, I'm a linguist; I'm going to apply Miller's Law here. Let's just assume for the moment that the answer is *yes.* Let's assume that the man who says his wife is wrong simply because she's arguing with *him,* regardless of the facts of the matter, is speaking the truth. What then, would this apply to?

That's easily answered. It would apply to every marriage in which the man's wisdom is so awesome that the wife can be *absolutely certain* that whatever he says will always and without exception be the best possible right thing to say. Notice, however, that exploring that hypothetical situation leads us immediately into a paradox. Because no man who is that wise would ever say (or think) anything so foolish as "You're wrong because you're arguing with *me*—never mind the facts or the circumstances."

Whether the model by which your household runs is the military one, with the husband as captain and the wife as first mate, or the full partnership model with husband and wife as coequals, this will be true. God knows everything and cannot make a mistake; human beings, lacking divine wisdom, must learn to reason together. They must listen, with full attention, to one another; they must speak one another's language; they must learn that winning and losing are irrelevant to their communication; and they must refrain from setting up and maintaining hostility loops in their language interactions.

Suppose you are a man in whose household St. Paul's rule is the one that applies. You are in charge. All the more reason for you to use the techniques in this book in your communication with your wife. You wouldn't let spoiled food or polluted water or toxic chemical wastes pile up in your home and poison her; it's your job to *defend* her (and anyone else in your household) against such things. It's equally your responsibility to defend against hostile language, which is every bit as poisonous.

Suppose that you are a woman in that household; your husband is in charge. All the more reason for you to use the techniques in this book in your communication with him. He is in just as much danger from hostile language as you are, whether he is attacking or responding to an attack from you. The stuff is toxic when it's in the air or the mind, no matter what its source. To participate in verbal slapfests with him puts his health, both physical and mental, at risk!

There are two additional compelling reasons why both members of a couple need to maintain a language environment free of violence. The first is that verbal violence is where physical violence begins. Sane adults don't just walk up to others and start hitting; first, there are hostile words. The possibility that the conflict will escalate to physical slaps, instead of verbal ones, must always be remembered.

The second reason applies when there are children in the home. It's easy to blame the violence we so deplore in our youngsters today on the influence of the media, but it's not the media's fault. The Bible contains violent language and narrative, but exposure to it—even very heavy and constant exposure—has never yet sent packs of teenagers out roaming the streets looking for sleeping men through whose foreheads they could drive spikes. It's not the violence the children observe that does the harm, it's the message the children get that adults in our culture *approve* of that violence. True, we say we don't approve, and sometimes— for example, with regard to violent rock music lyrics—we seem to mean it. But adults write and publish and film and market and purchase—and read, and watch—the foul flood of violent media products. This is true for every form of violence, from the trashtalk television shows to the films about chainsaw massacres and serial killers. Instead of saying, "The media made them do it!" we need to face two facts:

1. We're giving our children the message that although we expect them to pay lip service to peace, we really think that violence is exciting and interesting and worth our hard-earned money and time. Even on the shows where no one lays a hostile hand on anyone else, the character with the meanest mouth gets all the laughs.

2. Children who observe violence between their parents, either physical or verbal, grow up to believe that violence is the appropriate response to disagreement. Often they go on to perpetuate the cycle of violence in *their* homes, with *their* families. Your communication is the model your children use to learn language strategies for dealing with

conflict, and you are responsible to them as well as to one another.

All these reasons hold, you see, *long* before it ever becomes necessary to consider the commandment to turn the other cheek. When your stewardship of the language environment in your marriage and in your home is properly carried out, situations that pose that dilemma will be rare. St. Paul would be pleased.

WORKOUT SECTION

1. Talking to others isn't our only source of hostile language; we also have to deal with our stream of *self*-talk. We fuss at ourselves in the harshest and most judgmental ways, such as *"BOY, that was stupid! No WONDER nobody likes me! What a DUMMY I am!"* When you catch yourself doing that, tell yourself firmly to *stop* and take immediate action to occupy your mind in some more wholesome way. We also let unpleasant encounters with others run like endless loop tapes in our heads, going over them again and again. This input is just as toxic as it was when we heard it for the first time in the external world. So what are you to do when you have handled a disagreement well and avoided a fight—and you're still angry? What do you do when you've kept your anger to yourself because you realize that it's excessive or unjustified or flat out ridiculous—and you're still angry?

You have an alternative to either dumping this sort of linguistic trash on others or inflicting it on your self. You can keep it from piling up in your mind and doing you harm by writing it down *as a letter to the person you're angry with*. Get it all out of your system; say all the things you know you shouldn't say. But don't put it in your Conflict Journal! Write it all down, as a way of taking out the trash, and then *throw it away*. If writing is something you dislike so much that doing this would only increase your stress, put the letter on tape and then throw the tape away.

2. Begin keeping records of your verbal altercations in your Conflict Journal, in the form a reporter would use. Be as accurate as you can, but don't worry about perfection; you're not trying to create great literature, you're just observing your language environment and keeping an informal record of what happens there. Use the skills you've learned from this book to do a brief analysis. Here's a hypothetical example.

March 3, 1997, around 7:00 P.M.

I was writing a check at the supermarket when the woman in line behind me said, "If you'd filled in all but the total BEFORE they rang it up, the REST of us might've had a chance to get HOME sometime tonight!" I was so surprised I couldn't think of anything to say for a minute; I just stared at her. And then I said, "YOU have a lot of NERVE—and NO MANners!" and I slammed my check down on the counter, grabbed my groceries, and stalked out of there. I could hear her telling the clerk what a creep I was, all the way to the door.

> *Analysis:* The woman started Blaming at me, and I Blamed right back. It started a fight, the way Blaming at a Blamer always does. And then I left the checkout clerk and the other people in line to deal with it! I give myself a D on this one.

---

3. One very useful way to practice the Satir Mode skills is to take an example of one of the modes and "translate" it into all the others except Distracting. For example, suppose you've heard someone use the following Blaming utterance:

Blaming:

"WHY IS it that EVERY time I COME here I have to wait for HOURS?? MY time is important TOO, you know!"

You could rewrite that sequence in the other three modes like this:

Placating:

"Oh, I WISH I knew why I always have to wait for HOURS every time I COME here! Not that I have anything IMPOR-TANT to do, but STILL, doesn't MY time matter at ALL?"

Computing:

"No one enjoys waiting for hours every time they go to a place, as if their time had no value. Knowing why it happens might be helpful."

Leveling:

"Every time I come here I have to wait for hours. It makes me very angry. Is it necessary?"

Keep your "translations" in your Conflict Journal so that you can go back and revise them if better versions occur to you.

4. It's also helpful to practice the techniques in this book with other people. The best way to do role-playing exercises is with a group of three: two speakers (opener and responder) and an observer. Speaker 1 throws out an opening utterance that's an example of one or more language behavior modes; Speaker 2 recognizes the Satir Mode being used (or the sensory mode, or both); Speaker 2 responds according to the rules; the observer then offers appropriate comments about what happened. You need an observer so that the speakers can concentrate on what they're doing without having to also try to *remember* the exchange; if no observer is available, it's best to tape the role-playing and review it afterward. Change roles frequently so that everyone has a chance to play each role. And keep firmly in mind the fact that this *is* role-playing; it's neither contest nor combat. If the participants lose track of that fact, take a break.

5. I mentioned in the introduction that we have to try to understand the English of the Bible with almost no information except the words. Sometimes there are hints about body language, but much of the time all we have to go on is "And [the person] said . . ." Does that make a difference, do you think? In what way? Read some examples of quoted biblical speech and consider the question carefully.

THOUGHT BITES

1. "Unless you, or someone dear to you, has been the victim of terrible physical violence, chances are the worst pains you have suffered in life have come from words used cruelly—from ego-destroying criticism, excessive anger, sarcasm, public and private humiliation, hurtful nicknames, betrayal of secrets, rumors, and malicious gossip" (Telushkin, "Words," 1996, 2).

2. "The Christian's job is simply to bear witness to the truth, and to do that you first have to get within speaking distance of those who need to hear the truth, which is to say you try to enter into conversation. . . . Conversation requires civility" (Neuhaus, "We Can Get Along," 1996, 32).

3. "The freedom which Jesus offers is not the power to do with oneself and one's life whatever one wants; rather, it is the freedom to live as He lived" (Navrone, *Seeking God,* 1990, 22).

4. Communication "refers back to what has been said, points forward to what will be said, and is surrounded by the glow of what the speakers do not say but is nonetheless part of their communication" (Wren, *God Talk,* 1991, 74).

5. "The heart of the problem is not that Jesus was a man but that more men are not like Jesus" (Johnston, *She Who Is,* 1993, 161).

CHAPTER FIVE

SPEAKING OUT: CORRECTING A WRONG

Train up a child in the way he should go,
And when he is old he will not depart from
it.

Proverbs 22:6

The quotation is clear enough in its statement of the *goal* we should set for ourselves with regard to children: To bring them up, to raise them, in the way they should go. We know what "the way they should go" means, too. It means following the commandments—including the discomforting ones about turning the other cheek and returning good for evil—and living the Christian life. The problem, and the source of conflicts that can tear families and schools apart, is not in the *what* but in the *how*. Ideally the parents' and teachers' roles would be to provide wisdom, by specific instruction and by good example. But serving as a good example means doing all those things that seem so impossible in today's world, and the temptation to fall back on "Do as

I say, not as I do!" is very strong. And Proverbs tells us that wisdom comes from "the rod and reproof." This can lead to many difficult situations.

SCENARIO FIVE

Frank Sutter had been enjoying himself; the church picnic reminded him of other good times when he was a child. He was just getting up to go help himself to more fried chicken and potato salad when he heard an angry shout behind him and recognized the voice of his son-in-law, Lew Marks. Frank whirled around just in time to hear more shouting— "You watch your MOUTH when you talk to me! Don't you DARE tell me you won't do what I've told you to do!"—and see Lew lay a stinging slap right across fifteen-year-old Tommy's face.

Lew's arm was pulled back to add a second slap to the first when Frank grabbed it and held on tight. "**Lew!**" he said urgently, hoping that the people nearby hadn't had a clear view of what happened. "Cut it out! What's the **matter** with you?" And he jerked his head at the teenager, whose face was marked with what nobody could mistake for anything but the print of a strong and angry hand. "Go on, Tommy," he told his grandson, "go find your mother! I want to talk to your dad for a minute."

"Tommy, you stay right where you are!" Lew ordered in a steely voice. "**Don't you move from that spot!**"

"Lew, please—"

"Frank, I have all the respect in the world for you," Lew interrupted. "But you have no right to interfere when I am disciplining my son, and I won't tolerate it."

"But, Lew," Frank protested, "what you did then was just plain **wicked**! I don't know what Tommy did, but you didn't have to **hit** him like that! You can't DO that!"

Lew Marks raised both his hands like a traffic cop stopping an oncoming car. "Hold it right there!" he said coldly. "The **Bible** tells us what to do with a boy like Tommy, Frank. Proverbs 23:14 says, 'You shall beat him with a rod, and deliver his soul from hell.' And that's what I'm trying to do. Don't tell **me** I'm doing wrong, because the instructions **I'm** following come straight from the Almighty! Where'd you get **yours**?"

In the silence, Tommy spoke for the first time, and his voice was full of bitter sarcasm. "You're wasting your time trying to talk to him, Granddad," he said. "After all, he's got **God** on **his** side!"

Frank braced for the blow he was sure was coming, but Lew must have been embarrassed by the audience their disagreement had drawn; he turned to the boy and said, "You go to the car and stay there till your mother and I come—I'll deal with **you** when we get **home**. Go **on**, now!" And then he turned back to his father-in-law.

"Well, Frank?" he said. "Are you prepared to explain to me why I shouldn't obey God's word?"

Frank swallowed hard. *What could he say?* He needed a verse that would contradict the "spare the rod and spoil the child" verses, or one he could use to claim those words were meant for another day and age. But his mind was a blank. If there was a verse that said anything even remotely like "Be gentle and tender with your child," he couldn't remember it. And he *wasn't* prepared to stand up in front of people at a church picnic and appear to be telling his son-in-law to ignore the Bible!

Despising himself, hating Lew for putting him in such an impossible bind, and sick at heart, he turned his back without another word and walked away.

WHAT'S GOING ON HERE?

This kind of confrontation is one every Christian dreads. You observe something that you're convinced is wrong, and you feel obligated to speak out against it; and then the person you see as the wrongdoer uses the Bible as authority for the act—and you find yourself at a complete loss! It's worse when the dispute is over something as serious as striking a child, but even when the issue is trivial, the *situation* isn't. All the choices seem like bad ones. When you can't think of a verse that takes your side, any argument you raise implies that you think the Bible is in error. When you *can* think of one, it sounds as if you're claiming that the Bible contradicts itself. Few things are more ridiculous than two people throwing dueling Bible verses at each other! What are we to do?

POINTS OF VIEW

We all know what the points of view in this scenario are. Frank feels that it's his duty and his moral obligation to do and say what he did and said, and he feels that he failed in carrying out that duty. Lew feels equally certain that his moral obligation is to do what *he* did and said. But he not only doesn't feel like a failure, he feels like a winner. As for Tommy, he sees himself as helpless in the face of adult power. And the bystanders? Their point of view is that they wish none of this had happened, or—failing that—that someone among them had been wise enough to set matters right.

My personal opinion as a linguist is that the "rod" in the verses usually quoted should be understood today as a metaphor, not a literal rod; and I notice that even the literalists are willing to accept it as including fists and open hands and paddles of various kinds, none of *them* literal rods either. Dr. Brian Newman, in *The Father Book,* reminds us that when Proverbs was written the rod was "a shepherd's tool used for more than just discipline. The shepherd used it to guide his sheep and protect them" (1992, 89).

I believe the Bible is telling us that sparing the *discipline and guidance* spoils the child, not ordering us to hit our kids. Metaphors are everywhere in the Bible, and that rod is just another one, like "You are the salt of the earth" and many thousands more. I'm equally convinced that the Bible's term *reproof* doesn't mean verbal *abuse*. But that makes me no less at a loss for wisdom in situations like the one in Scenario Five.

All that said, two things relevant to this problem are items about which there can be no question whatsoever:

1. The wisest course anyone can follow in raising children is to raise them in such a way that the rod—literal or figurative—won't be needed.
2. The wisest course anyone can follow for handling arguments like the one between Lew and Frank is to communicate in such a way that the argumenmt is headed off before it can begin.

An ounce of prevention truly is worth a pound—several pounds— of cure. The techniques you've been learning in this book are all designed to help you provide that critical ounce in your own language environment, honorably and with no sacrifice of principles or dignity. In the section that follows, we'll look at another such technique, called the *three-part message*.

A COMMUNICATION TECHNIQUE: USING THREE-PART MESSAGES

Often we have no idea who first discovered or devised a particular communication technique; the information about using the sensory modes is like that. Other techniques (the Satir Modes, for example, or Miller's Law) have clear, recorded beginnings. The three-part message falls in between. It began as the traditional two-part "I-message," which has been used so long that no one seems to know who first suggested it. The third part was added by effectiveness expert Thomas Gordon, and I (and others) have since made a few modifications.

One of the things we know with certainty about communication in our culture is that no adult likes to be told what to do or how to be. We have a knee-jerk, negative reaction to such messages, even when we know we're in the wrong (perhaps *especially* when we know we're in the wrong). This negative attitude toward commands and criticism begins in earliest childhood and grows stronger over the years. It appears fiercer in teenagers than in most adults, because the youngsters' typical lack of self-control makes their reactions so obvious. But this is misleading. Adults, when speaking honestly, will tell you that in most situations they greatly dislike being told what to do and have a hard time giving such messages a fair and objective hearing.

Because "what to do" and "how to be" messages are an inescapable part of our lives, we need a way to construct them that will help us get *past* the automatic resistance and resentment they typically evoke. The three-part message is the best tool for that purpose. Here's the pattern:

When you _____, I feel _____, because _____.
       1   2   3

Example:
When you don't water the tomatoes, I feel angry, because plants die without water.

A two-part I-Message would be either "I feel angry when you don't water the tomatoes" or "When you don't water the tomatoes, I feel angry." It identifies the specific item of behavior the speaker wants changed and the emotion the speaker feels about that behavior, stating them in either order depending on the emphasis desired. That's a good beginning, and there are times when it's as far as you can go. But the added third part strengthens the message by adding to it the real-world consequence or fact *that is a justification for the utterance and explains why the speaker feels entitled to say it.* Ideally, none of the three parts is anything that a rational person would argue about. And I feel that it's best to say the "When" section first, because that puts the focus where it's most appropriate: squarely on the item of behavior.

There's nothing difficult about constructing a three-part message if you yourself understand what you're trying to say. It's easy to understand why the example above has a better chance of being heard objectively than the more typical "When you act like you have **no** responsibility for any of the garden work around here, it makes me so mad I can't **stand** it, and I'm NOT going to put UP with it any longer, do you **hear me**?" Simple, and obvious, right? Right. Nevertheless, I recommend that when you have any lead time before offering commands or criticism, you write down your three-part message in advance and make certain that it has all its parts in good order and that it follows the pattern exactly.

First, you identify the exact item of behavior you're going to comment on, and state it. That means setting aside "When you act the way you do," and "When you behave like you were emperor of the world," and "When you treat me like dirt," and "When you're disrespectful," and "When your work isn't as good as it ought to be," and so on—because such sequences are hopelessly vague. When parents ask me for help with a rebellious child, I always ask if they're sure the youngster knows what the problem is, and they usually say, "Yes, of course!" But when I ask the child, "Do you know why your parents are so angry?"

the answer is almost always, "Sure—because I'm no **good**!" or "Sure—because they **hate** me!" It's important to be *specific*. If you don't know what it is you want, how can you expect your listener to know?

Next, you identify the emotion you feel, and state that. Just say "I feel . . ." and fill in with "angry" or "distressed" or "worried" or whatever is the truth. Don't change it to "you make me feel," or "it makes me feel." Set aside "I feel like it means you don't respect me," and "I feel like you were trying to hurt me" and all the rest. The pattern is "I feel" plus the emotion felt, nothing more. The only change that is safe is to use Computer Mode here and word part two as "People feel" or "Teachers feel" or whatever fits the circumstances. Sometimes that can be a very good idea, either because you're acting on behalf of someone else or because you want to decrease the tension and defuse hostility.

Finally—and this is usually the hardest part—identify the real-world consequence or fact that gives you the right to speak on the matter. There are times when it seems to you that the only possible way to fill in part three will be "Because I'm the grown-up," or "Because I'm the boss." But such cases represent the use of *force;* they mean "Because I have the power to punish you if you don't do what I say, and I'm prepared to use that power." They should be the *last* resort, always! When people go along with what you say only because they fear punishment, they will do so as reluctantly and inadequately as they dare, and their *attitude* about the matter not only will not change but will be hardened by their resentment of you. And "Because I say so!" is absolutely not part of any well-made three-part message. In the tomato example, part three says "because plants die without water." No one can argue about that; it's a concrete fact, verifiable in the real world, and entirely independent of the personal power of the speaker. That's how it should be.

Remember: We aren't forbidden to be angry. What's forbidden is anger that is excessive or unjustified or thoughtless. When you can't fill in all three parts of a three-part message properly, that's strong evidence that you don't have enough information—or perhaps enough wisdom—to know whether your anger is any of those unacceptable things or *not*. In such cases, the three-part message can prevent you from making a serious mistake.

A satisfactory three-part message lets you provide specific instruction and a good example at the same time. It lets you request some change in your listener, some improvement, some *difference* from the status quo, without speaking harshly or threatening reprisal. That is one of the ways to set a good example. What you say may be reproof, but it is not verbal abuse. It is the rod that guides and defends, not the rod that beats. The more you write out such messages in advance the more likely it is that when you find yourself needing to produce one "off the top of your head" you'll be able to do that successfully.

People sometimes say to me, "But I shouldn't **have** to bother with all that! There shouldn't be any question about what I say, because I'm in charge, and what I say **goes**!" That's one way to run a home or business or church or organization, certainly. But it is more properly a way to run a *war*. In combat the commander must be able to state an order and know that it will be instantly obeyed without question; otherwise, people will get killed. Homes and businesses and churches and organizations don't have to be run that way, and should not be. Except in combat and in life-or-death emergencies, such a regime is as far from loving your neighbor as yourself as you can get.

In Scenario Five there were no three-part messages. Lew and Frank were just laying down the law for Tommy and for one another. Let's go back and change that; let's find out how using three-part messages could have improved the situation.

ANOTHER LOOK
AT SCENARIO FIVE

Suppose that in Scenario Five Frank Sutter had been familiar with the three-part message technique. Would he have been able to handle his interaction with his son-in-law more successfully? Suppose that Lew Marks had known about the three-part message; might he then have been able to discipline Tommy without resorting to physical or verbal violence?

FRANK'S ENCOUNTER WITH LEW

Let's go back to the first moment in the interaction between Frank and Lew, when the slap had already happened. This was Frank's opening line:

"**Lew!** Cut it out! What's the **matter** with you?"

We can understand why Frank did this. He was taken by surprise and was horrified by what he'd seen and heard; he didn't stop to think. But a complaint that begins like this one almost always fails. When such openings do work, it's ordinarily because the listener *fears* the speaker, and such compliance, given under duress, will always be grudging and temporary. That outcome should be your communication goal *only* when the command is literally a split-second matter of life and death, like shouting at someone to duck as a rock hurtles toward his head—in that case, if he does duck, you've succeeded! Such cases are rare.

We're not used to consciously choosing our *communication goals* before we begin talking. We have to *learn* to do that. And it's never more important than when, as is true for Frank, a strong emotion may be interfering with our ability to think clearly. For Frank Sutter, three plausible goals exist:

1. To express his feelings and get them off his chest so that he'll feel less frustrated by them;
2. To inform and educate Lew; to, as the catchphrase has it, "raise Lew's consciousness;"
3. To persuade Lew to change the behavior Frank objects to.

This is the typical set of goals in situations of this kind. If Frank chooses Goal 1, it makes very little difference what he says, as long as he feels better afterward. If he chooses Goal 2, he has to take time to construct a careful case, based on strong arguments and solid facts; he can't just wing it. If he chooses Goal 3, his best strategy is to use a three-part message, in either Leveler or Computer Mode:

Frank: "Lew, when you slap Tommy's face, I feel distressed, because physical blows of that kind are dangerous." [Leveling]

Frank: "Lew, when someone slaps a child's face, people feel distressed, because physical blows of that kind are dangerous." [Computing]

Now Frank hasn't given Lew a direct order, he hasn't *judged* Lew, and he has not challenged Lew's character or sanity. The message itself, in either Satir Mode, is well put together. The slap did take place, which verifies the first part; the distress is obvious, in Frank and in bystanders, verifying the second part. And although some people may disagree about how dangerous it is to slap a youngster, there is considerable consensus on Frank's side about part three.

Whenever the goal is to change a behavior, a well-made three-part message like the two examples above is by *far* the best move. Whether you use Leveling or Computing should depend on the circumstances at the time. As always, when Leveling is safe and appropriate, it's the best choice. However, if feelings are running extremely high, if you know that your listener is overly touchy and defensive, or if you're delivering the message on someone else's behalf, choose Computer Mode.

Lew's response to the three-part message can't be predicted with certainty. He *could* say exactly what he said in the original version of the scenario. But the communication situation—the language environment in which the encounter takes place—is now dramatically different.

When Lew is given a direct order by another adult, in front of his son (and, in this case, in public as well), a strong negative reaction is guaranteed, because he has been backed into a corner and risks losing face in a way he may not be able to accept. When Frank's objection comes as one of the suggested three-part messages, however, a substantial chance exists that Lew will react far less violently. Even if he still insists on a fight, chances are good that he'll argue about whether slaps are or are not dangerous to a child, and that should keep him from moving immediately to Bible verses for his defense. This would give Frank a better environment for persuasion.

LEW'S ENCOUNTER WITH TOMMY

It's probable that this unfortunate incident could have been avoided altogether by using a three-part message. We know that Lew had given Tommy a direct order of some kind and that the boy had refused to obey it. Suppose Tommy wanted to go eat with friends, instead of staying with his parents. Here's the probable original dialogue:

Lew: "Hey, Tommy . . . where are you going, son?"
Tommy: "I'm gonna go eat with my friends, Dad, okay?"

Lew: "**No,** it's **not** okay! You stay right here and eat with
your mother and me!"

Tommy: "Aw, Dad, come **on**! That's not—"

Lew: "That's ENOUGH! I don't want to hear another word
OUT of you!"

Tommy: "But—"

Lew: "I said you'll eat with US! Case closed!"

Tommy: "I'm not gonna do it! And YOU CAN'T MAKE me!"

Lew: "You watch your MOUTH when you talk to me!
Don't you DARE tell me you won't do what I've told
you to do!" [He slaps Tommy, hard.]

After that dialogue, the disagreement between Frank and Lew
would surely follow. Here, for comparison, is a revision in which
Lew Marks is familiar with the technique for using three-part
messages. We'll also tone down the hostility in his voice (indicated above by bold type and capital letters), since someone skilled
in techniques like the three-part message will rarely consider an
open attack stance a good way to begin an interaction.

Lew: "Hey, Tommy . . . where are you going, son?"

Tommy: "I'm gonna go eat with my friends, Dad, okay?"

Lew: "No, it's not okay. Your mother and I would like for
you to stick around and eat with us."

Tommy: "Aw, Dad . . . I don't want to do that!"

Lew: "Tommy, when you tell me you don't want to eat sup-
per with us, I feel sad, because meals are just about
the only chance our family has to spend time
together these days."

Tommy: [Sighs.] "I guess that's true."

Lew: "You eat with Mom and me, and then you can go
spend the rest of the evening with your friends. Fair

enough?"

Tommy: "Yeah. Okay—that's fair."

I'm not claiming that a three-part message will magically turn a bad relationship between parent and child into a storybook relationship. If Lew and Tommy have been getting along badly for a long time and there's a lot of bad blood between them, this might not help. Tommy might refuse to negotiate, might continue to be hostile, might still defy his father and have to be punished in some way. But there's nothing *unlikely* about the revision I've just offered you; over the course of the past quarter century I have seen hundreds of such interactions go exactly that well. And the earlier a parent or other caregiver begins using three-part messages instead of more typical hasty complaints and criticism, the more likely it is that the development of a *combat* relationship between adult and child can be prevented.

Before we leave this topic, I want to assure you that finding yourself unable to complete the third part of a three-part message—the most common problem—doesn't mean that you have to keep silent. You can still use a two-part I-message. Frank could have said simply, "Lew, when you slap Tommy's face, I feel distressed" (or angry or appalled). Or, in Computer Mode, "When someone slaps a child's face, people feel . . ." that emotion. The difference is that the I-message is less likely to persuade people to change their behavior, because it leaves open the question of why you feel that you're justified in asking for the change. It may still be a good idea for you to let them *know* how you feel.

WORKOUT SECTION

1. Set up two pages in your Conflict Journal for recording data about criticism and commands, and responses to them, in your language environment. One should just be a record of such items that occur around you, including those that you yourself originate; write it as a simple list: "3/5/97—Mr. Clayton said, 'Tomorrow, get here by seven.' I said, 'I will if I can.' He said, **'Don't** argue, just **get** here!' I said nothing, and I got there at seven the next day—but I got there mad." The other page should look like this:

Three-Part Messages Log
Date and Time

Situation:

The three-part message that I delivered:

The response I got:

What I said next:

What was said to me next:

What happened: [That is, whether the requested change or action was agreed to, whether it took place, how you and the other person felt about it, so far as you could tell, and so on.]

---

2. Identify the ten or so criticisms you would most like to make but haven't been able or willing to make, and write them out as three-part messages. They can be directed at the president, your local police department, or anyone else, living or dead.

3. Three-part messages are also an excellent way to deliver *praise*. That may seem strange at first, but consider the linguistic facts: both negative criticism and praise have as a metamessage "I am qualified to make judgments about you and speak to you about my conclusions." Furthermore, many people are suspicious of praise and afraid that there's "a catch." Try writing some three-part praise messages; try *using* some. Here's an example:

"When you get an A in algebra, I'm pleased, because your teacher tells me that an A in that subject is rare."

4. When you're angry with someone, but you're not sure why, try to write a three-part message; sometimes that will make your own feelings and motivations clear to you, even if you don't ever deliver the message. Similarly, when someone you're on a reasonably good footing with is angry with *you* and you don't know why, explain about the three-part message and ask her— In private, and at her convenience—to write a message like that for you. (Anyone who speaks English will understand the tomato plant example that began this chapter.)

THOUGHT BITE

1. "The stereotypical father is stern and judgmental. The real father is also tender and merciful. The stereotype is strong. The real father tempers that strength with control" (Minirth et al., *The Father Book*, 1992, 26).

Assuming that control can only come from the power of superior force is a common error. Control also comes from having adequate information and realizing that force isn't necessary.

CHAPTER SIX

DELIVERING
BAD NEWS
AT WORK

Wisdom is found on the lips of him who has understanding.

Proverbs 10:13

Giving someone bad news is one of the hardest communication tasks we ever have to face. There are rare individuals who seem to *enjoy* doing that, but most of us feel deeply distressed when we have to be the bearers of bad tidings. And that distress can interfere with our communication skills at the very time when we most badly need for those skills to be at their peak.

SCENARIO SIX

Hal Johnson enjoyed being a high school counselor. His job gave him many opportunities to make positive contributions to the lives of young people. But it also included a task he hated: breaking bad news to parents. His meeting today with Brenda

Marks, who was a friend of his from church, was that kind of occasion, and he had been dreading it. He'd gone over and over it in his head, weighing the different ways he could approach it, and nothing he'd come up with had satisfied him. It was going to be awkward, and he was nervous about it, but there was no way to put it off any longer. It had to be done.

"Hello, Brenda," he said as she came into his office. "Thank you for coming in so promptly! Please sit down; I'll close this door and be right with you."

He sat down at his desk, opened the file in front of him, and took a deep breath—but Brenda spoke before he could begin.

"I suppose you want to talk to me about **Tommy!**" she said, her voice tense and strained.

"Yes, as a matter of fact I do," he answered. "I see **that** doesn't surprise you!"

"What's **that** supposed to mean?" she snapped, but she didn't wait for him to answer; she went right on. "Hal, Tommy's a **good** child! If you could hear him talk about how much he wants to do well, how much he wants to do something **important** with his life. . . . It breaks my heart. He's only **fifteen!** All his problems right now ought to be **trivial** ones!"

"I'm afraid I can't see what Tommy's been doing lately as **trivial**," Hal said bluntly. "From **my** point of view, you and Lew are looking at real **trouble!**"

Brenda looked straight at him, her chin high. "Now you listen to **me**, Hal!" she said defiantly. "I **warn** you: I'm not prepared to sit here and hear you bad-mouth my son! You can just—"

"Brenda," Hal broke in, "I know how things look to you. You love your boy, and in your eyes he can do no wrong. That's natural; I see it all the time. But this is something you **have** to **know!** Tommy was late to school yesterday morning, and—"

"So he was **late**! Now I've heard **everything**! **You've** called me in here just because Tommy was—"

Hal's patience was exhausted; the struggle just to get the woman's attention was more than he could deal with. "**Look, Brenda**," he interrupted, "can't you see I'm trying to tell you something **important**? When Tommy finally arrived yesterday, it wasn't just that he was late! His teacher only needed one **look** to see that he'd been **drink**ing!"

Brenda went white, and she stood up abruptly. "How **dare** you say that about my child!" she hissed at him. "How **dare** you!"

"**Wait** a minute, Brenda!" Hal answered, startled. "I'm saying it because it's **true**! And you and I and Lew have to decide how best to **deal** with it! You see, teenage drinking is—"

"I know my **son**, Hal Johnson!" Brenda said, cutting him off sharply. "He's not perfect; I never claimed he was. But he would never, **never**, drink alcohol! And if you have anything **else** to say, you can say it to my **law**yer! I'll see **you** in **court**!"

And before he could make a sound, she had left his office, slamming the door furiously behind her.

What's Going on Here?

This mess isn't what Hal had planned or what he had expected. He'd planned to discuss Tommy's problems with his mother and offer some suggestions for solving them. Instead, he managed only to become involved in a serious and very unpleasant argument. Certainly he can take the position that he was only doing what his job required and what was best for the boy; he can claim that Brenda was way out of line and a classic case of someone blaming the messenger. But none of those things, however accurate they may be, is going to be any help to Tommy. And Brenda's behavior, however much it could be explained as due to shock and disbelief, has done nothing but add more problems to a situation that was bad enough already. The last thing a youngster in trouble needs is to have the adults who are responsible for him fighting among themselves.

POINTS OF VIEW

Brenda Marks's perception of this situation is focused on one single point: her fierce determination to protect her only child. Her husband is a stern man, inflexibly determined to rely on the most literal interpretation of "Spare the rod and spoil the child"; Tommy is always in trouble with his dad for one thing or another. And since he became a teenager he seems always to be in trouble elsewhere as well. Nothing really serious—just many little things, with the most usual complaint being that he has a bad attitude. Brenda is convinced that Tommy is a good kid, unjustly treated by the rest of the world, and she is not *about* to let him down. To her, Hal Johnson is just one more staff member at the school who dislikes her son and is ready to condemn him at the drop of a hat. When she says she doesn't believe the boy was drinking—meaning that his teacher was either lying or mistaken—she means it 100 percent. Her perception is that both she and Tommy have been attacked and abused, and she's prepared to fight back.

Hal Johnson has no idea what set Brenda off and made her so angry. As he sees it, all he did was fulfill his obligation to Tommy, to Tommy's parents, and to the school, by stating the simple truth. It seems to him that Brenda Marks's behavior was irrational, that she met his sincere attempt to help with insults and belligerence, and that he did nothing to deserve such treatment. The Marks family attends the same church the Johnsons go to, and he's aware of Lew's theories on child raising; that's why he asked only Brenda to come to school for a conference. Now he wonders if perhaps he's misjudged Lew. *Maybe Brenda is so overprotective of the boy that she spoils him. . . . Maybe Lew is just trying to counteract that spoiling.* He was prepared for Brenda to find it hard to believe him, as any mother might; he was prepared for shock and perhaps tears. But he did *not* expect to be verbally abused and threatened with a lawsuit, and he has no intention of taking either without a fight!

For Tommy's sake, the adults in this situation need to set aside their personal concerns and biases and find a way to help him. It's not likely that Brenda will really sue the school; once she's had a chance to calm down she'll realize how absurd that would be. But the atmosphere between family and school has now been so poisoned that setting things right won't be easy. It may be a long time before *Tommy's* needs get the careful attention they deserve. However, there's nothing wrong with either Hal's or Brenda's morals, character, or intentions. Hal's doing his best to be a good counselor; Brenda's doing her best to be a good mother. Despite the opinions the two now have of each other, the problems are not in the people, but in the language.

We've now examined four useful techniques for tackling problems of language and fixing them. In this review chapter, we're going to go back to the scenario and find out how using all those techniques in combination might have made the outlook for Tommy's future less gloomy. To get us started, let's bring together for review all the rules that we may need to refer to as we go along.

SUMMARY OF RULES

True Listening, Using Miller's Law

In order to understand what another person is saying . . .

Assume that it is true.

Try to imagine what it could be true of.

Give the person speaking to you your full attention.

Using the Sensory Modes

Match the sensory mode coming at you, if you can.

Otherwise, try to use no sensory language at all.

Using the Satir Modes

If you want what's happening to escalate, match the Satir Mode coming at you.

Otherwise—or if you're not sure what to do—go to Computer Mode and stay there until you have a reason to change.

Using the Three-Part Message

In order to deliver a message of command or criticism, use the following pattern, filling the blanks with items that are concrete and verifiable:

"When you [*exact item of behavior*],

I feel [*emotion*],

because [*real-world consequence or fact that justifies the utterance*]." (Leveling)

or

"When you/when someone [*exact item of behavior*],

people feel [*emotion*],

because [*real-world consequence or fact that justifies the utterance*]." (Computing)

Your goal in following these rules is to establish and maintain a language environment in which verbal abuse and hostile language are extremely *rare,* with no sacrifice of the dignity or principles of anyone involved. Not only because that is the description for a wholesome language environment—a desirable goal in itself—but also so that the need to make decisions about turning the other cheek just doesn't arise. This allows you to be a good steward of the reserves of moral strength you need to be able to call upon in situations of real crisis.

Now let's go back to the scenario and see what we can do to improve the communication that takes place there.

Another Look at Scenario Six: Combining the Four Techniques

We're going to go through the dialogue from the scenario now, sequence by sequence, to identify the strategic errors that were made and decide what the speakers could have done to avoid or repair them.

If we were carrying out a task like this for a broken machine, it would be an orderly process. We would just do step one, and then step two, and so on to the end, and we could predict with reasonable accuracy what would happen at each stage. There would be only a limited number of possibilities after each adjustment we made. Language interactions aren't like that. Every small change you make opens up an infinite number of possible new circumstances, and all the changes interact. However, the popular impression that communication is more or less a random phenomenon isn't correct either. We'll keep this analysis and revision as tidy as possible. Here's the original opening sequence:

Hal: "Hello, Brenda. Thank you for coming in so promptly! Please sit down; I'll close this door and be right with you."

Brenda: [Tensely.] "I suppose you want to talk to me about **Tom**my!"

Hal: "Yes, as a matter of fact, I do. I see **that** doesn't surprise you!"

Already these two are off to a bad start, with mistakes on both sides of the interaction. Brenda's wary opening line alerts Hal to the fact that she has arrived with negative expectations about what's coming. And Hal, instead of continuing with the courteous tone he set in his greeting, matches her negative for negative. "I see **that** doesn't surprise you!" is just sarcastic enough to accomplish that. The two have now set up a hostility loop, which Brenda proceeds to feed. The next two lines in the scenario are a straightforward exchange of open Blaming.

Brenda: [Snaps at him.] "What's **that** supposed to mean? Hal, Tommy's a **good** child! If you could hear him talk about how much he wants to do well, how much he wants to do something **important** with his life. . . . It breaks my heart. He's only fif**teen**! All his problems right now ought to be **trivial** ones!"

Hal: "I'm afraid I can't see what Tommy's been doing lately as **triv**ial! From **my** point of view, you and Lew are looking at real **troub**le!"

You will have noticed that Brenda is hearing dominant and Hal is sight dominant; and because both have become tense and defensive, they've stopped speaking the same language. Their sensory-modes mismatch increases their tension, locking them ever more tightly into their dominant modes, which makes the tension worse, and so on around the loop. The mismatch continues all the way to the end of the argument. And neither one of these people is listening to the other; they're hearing, but they're not listening. Here's the next sequence:

Brenda: [Defiantly.] "Now you listen to **me**, Hal! I **warn** you: I'm not prepared to sit here and listen to you bad-mouth my son! You can just—"

Hal: "Brenda, I know how things look to you. You love your boy, and in your eyes he can do no wrong. That's natural; I see it all the time. But this is something you **have** to **know**! Tommy was late to school yesterday morning, and—"

Brenda: "So he was **late**! Now I've heard **every**thing! **You've** called me in here just because Tommy was—"

A number of counterproductive things are now going on:

- The hostility is escalating because both Hal and Brenda are vigorously feeding the hostility loop.
- Understanding is being made impossible because neither party is listening to the other. And because both are using Miller's-Law-in-Reverse, instantly rejecting what the other person says as false and leaping to conclusions about the motives for saying it.
- Both speakers are cutting each other off with abrupt interruptions.
- Both are using conflicting sensory modes: sight mode for Hal, hearing mode for Brenda.
- Both are making all the wrong Satir Mode choices, matching every Blaming utterance with a Blaming response.
- All the criticisms and requests for change are being given the most negative form possible, short of resorting to primitive measures like name-calling and obscenities. No three-part messages here!

All these errors are going on, interactively and synergistically (that is, with the whole being more than the sum of its parts), at the same time. Turning the other cheek, returning good for evil, doesn't even appear to be part of the communication land-scape. Hal and Brenda obviously went straight to the Warrior metaphor as first resort, and both are determined to win. How could communication NOT break down?

At this point, we have a language interaction almost totally out of control. It's rushing toward an inevitable cliff—and it falls right over the edge.

Hal: "**Look**, Brenda, can't you see I'm trying to tell you something **important**? When Tommy finally arrived yesterday, it wasn't just that he was late! His teacher only needed one **look** to see that he'd been **drink-ing**!"

Brenda: [Standing up, white-faced.] "How **dare** you say that about my child! How **dare** you!"

Hal: "**Wait** a minute, Brenda! I'm saying it because it's **true**! And you and I and Lew have to decide how best to **deal** with it! You see, teenage drinking is—"

Brenda: "I know my **son**, Hal Johnson! He's not perfect; I never claimed he was! But he would never, **never** drink alcohol! And if you have anything **else** to say, you can say it to my **law**yer! I'll see **you** in **court**!" [Walks out, slamming the door.]

Hostile language in English is easy to identify because it has very predictable and obvious characteristics. We tend to believe that we identify it by the words used, but that's not accurate. For English, more than 90 percent of the *emotional* information is in the body language—especially the tone and intonation of the voice—rather than in the words. Here are the three defining char-acteristics of hostile English:

1. It uses very *personal* vocabulary—"I, me, you, this town, this church, that job of yours . . ." and the like.
2. It uses extra emphasis (called **stress**) on words and parts of words, shown in written speech by underlining, italics, capital letters, and descriptive sequences such as "she said angrily" or "he told her belligerently."
3. No alternative explanation for the presence of the first two characteristics is available. (Suppose someone is being rushed to emergency surgery, and a doctor running along beside the gurney says "QUICK! I have to know your BLOOD type!" That's not likely to be an example of hostile language. The emergency medicine context fully accounts for the personal vocabulary and the extra emphasis.)

When people who are distressed about others' speech tell them that "It wasn't what you said, it was the way you **said** it!" they are quite right. Any sequence of language that has these three characteristics, no matter how mild and inoffensive the words themselves may be in isolation, is hostile.

In analyzing Scenario Six we don't have to think hard to decide whether the three criteria are met. From the first line out of Brenda's mouth to the end of the interaction, both speakers rely on personal vocabulary and multiple emphatic stresses; and no explanation for what happened, other than the expression of hostility, exists. Neither Hal's nervousness about the encounter nor Brenda's concern for Tommy is a severe enough emergency to serve as an excuse for this barrage of verbal slaps and gouges, attacks and counterattacks; it was unnecessary.

How To Fix It

To fix the first sequence, either Hal has to change his language behavior, or Brenda does. For purposes of discussion, let's assume that Hal does the changing, because he is the trained professional. All he has to do is forego the sarcastic response he made in the original dialogue and continue his courtesy instead. Like this:

Hal: "Hello, Brenda. Thank you for coming in so promptly! Please sit down; I'll close this door and be right with you."

Brenda: [Tensely.] "I suppose you want to talk to me about Tommy!"

Hal: "That's right; I do."

One of the most puzzling things about helping people with communication problems is how *hard* it is to convince them that smart cracks—like "I see **that** doesn't surprise you!" with its metamessage about Tommy's constantly being in trouble—cause far more hassle than they're worth. People say things like "But a little humor is **always** a good idea!" and "A few little witty words like that couldn't **possibly** do any harm!" They're wrong. Despite the rounds of applause and laughter when smart cracks and put-downs are flying about in television sitcoms, the brief kick you get from a witty line in a tense situation will be paid for twice over in unpleasantness later. Brenda's opening makes it clear that she's tense and is expecting bad news about her child; all Hal has to do, and all he *should* do, is agree.

If that happens, everything changes. Because no hostility loop has been set up, Brenda has no *reason* to snap at the counselor or launch into her long, emotional speech defending Tommy. Instead, she will say something like this: "What did you want to tell me, Hal?" or "Why did you ask me to come in, Hal?" She will still sound tense, but she won't be angry. And now, if Hal is wise, his response will be . . .

Hal: "I'm afraid that you and Lew may be facing a serious situation, Brenda. I'd like to tell you about it."

If Hal does this, he has warned Brenda that what's coming next may be distressing and has asked her permission to go on. You've seen this small courtesy before, in earlier scenarios and dialogues. When transmitting negative messages that may come as a shock to your listener, or when you have reason to believe the listener may be emotionally fragile at least for the moment, this is a wise move.

Notice where this puts us in our analysis and revision. Because there's no hostility loop, Hal has no reason to be anything but mildly cautious (as he was initially), and this means that he won't be locked into sight mode. At this point, no sensory mode mismatch exists. But if Brenda becomes upset and emotional as in the original scenario, Hal's proper strategy is to match her sensory mode to reduce the level of tension and help her be more at ease. We'll follow that strategy.

Hal has asked Brenda's permission to go on, warning that it may be rough:

Brenda: "All right . . . What is it?"
Hal: "Brenda, we had a problem here yesterday morning. I'm very sorry to have to tell you that when Tommy got to school yesterday it was obvious to his teacher that he had been drinking. He was late; and somewhere between home and school he'd made an unwise decision."
Brenda: [White-faced.] "Hal, I know my son! He's not perfect; I've never claimed he was. But I **also** know he would never, **never**, drink alcohol! You've **got** to be WRONG!"

Hal: "It's hard for any parent to hear that a child is in trou-
           ble. The first thing a school does in such situations is
           check for other possible explanations, like illness or
           injury."
Brenda: "You **did that**? You **checked**?"
Hal: "Absolutely—and the problem was alcohol."

Notice what Hal does here. Because Brenda reacts so strongly
to the bad news, he shifts into Computer Mode and speaks as
neutrally as he can. His message is the same—he presents the
facts about what happened—but Computing language lowers the
emotional temperature. Talking about "any parent" and a hypothetical school makes the discussion more abstract, less personal,
and gives Brenda a little more space. The most likely outcome
is that she will respond by switching to Leveler Mode, like this:

Brenda: "I can't believe it, Hal. . . . I just can't!" [Eyes fill with
           tears.]
Hal: "I know it's difficult, Brenda. I'm sorry. But what
           Tommy said to us was, 'I only had a couple of beers!
           What's the big deal?' So we need to talk about it and
           decide what we can do to help your son. This is new
           behavior for him, not an established pattern. If we're
           careful, I'm sure everything will be all right."
Brenda: "Hal, I have to talk to Tommy and hear this for
           myself. I have to hear his side of it. And then I'll call
           you, right away, to talk about what happens next."
Hal: "That's fine with me, Brenda. I'll be waiting."
Brenda: "And Hal. . . . Thank you for letting me know."

Because Hal knows Brenda well, he was able to finish this
interaction in Leveler Mode. When he had no ready word or

phrase from the hearing vocabulary, he was careful to avoid sensory language completely. Because there was never a need for a command or criticism, he didn't have to use any three-part messages. But suppose that when Brenda said she'd talk to Tommy and then call about the next move, Hal might have had to refuse because of school rules. Then a three-part message would have been helpful:

Hal: "I wish I could say yes to that, Brenda. But when you say you'll talk to Tommy at home first, I feel concerned, because school regulations don't offer us that option."

Brenda: "What does that mean? What are we supposed to **do?**"

Hal: "Tommy's waiting in the principal's office. We have to talk to him together now and try to decide what to do next. Do you want to go down to the office and get him, or shall I call?"

Brenda: "I'll go. . . . That way, I can let him know I'm ready to listen to his side of this before he has to hear anything else."

Hal: "That's fine with me, Brenda. I'll be waiting."

Much hard work lies ahead for these people. Talking this over with Tommy is going to be difficult, especially if he is defensive and defiant. Talking to his father will be even worse; someone will surely have to try to convince Lew that hitting Tommy is as likely to drive him to alcohol as keep him away from it. But Hal and Brenda are prepared now to work together to help her troubled son, and no one is being distracted from that most urgent task by angry insults and threats. This is what you can expect when you add skilled communication techniques to the language abilities you're already blessed with.

I want to close this review by reminding you that, for English, it's not the words that carry most emotional messages. Messages such as "I'm angry" and "I'm frightened" and "I'm pleased" are carried not by the words but by the tunes that the words are set to. It's impossible to show a reader those tunes with the English writing system. Let's consider just one of Hal's lines in the revised dialogue above. Brenda asks if the school checked to be sure Tommy's problem couldn't have been explained in some other way, and Hal says . . .

"Absolutely—and the problem was alcohol."

Those words aren't magic. As written on the page, they have an amazing variety of possible meanings. You know of course that if the sentence were written like this—

"ABSOLUTEly! And the PROBlem was ALCOhol!"

—it would be a verbal slap. When you read it aloud, bearing down hard on the parts written all in capital letters and listening to the way it sounds, that's unmistakable. However, it's important to remember that the same words—spoken in an icy tone, or through clenched teeth, or with a facial expression of disgust—would also be blows aimed straight at the listener. That's why chronic verbal abusers feel comfortable offering excuses such as "But all I said was . . . ," followed by the words that have been objected to. They know that the tune they set those words to, the tune that would back up the objection, is no longer available as evidence; they can safely give the same words a neutral intonation and get away with it.

Several times each year I'm asked to serve as an expert witness for a claim of hostile and "improper" language, with my testimony to be based on a *written transcript* of the court proceedings. I have to refuse those requests, because it is literally impossible to reconstruct emotional messages from written language alone. I would have to have a videotape of the proceedings before I could make any statements that I'd be willing to swear were "the truth, the whole truth, and nothing but the truth." *No* word is inherently hostile. I can call you dreadful names so tenderly that you will immediately understand that their emotional message is "I love you dearly"; I can pay you extravagant compliments in such a sarcastic manner that you know I despise you. In either of those cases, a written transcript of my words would be totally misleading.

In all of the dialogue in this book, therefore, you should hear *neutral* intonation in your mind as you read the quoted speech where I haven't indicated any other kind. No communication technique, no choice of words, can overrule a hostile message that is given its surface shape by body language. People can listen carefully with an expression of hate and revulsion on their faces. They can match sensory modes with a sneer and respond to Blaming with sarcastic or viciously cold Computing; they can offer three-part messages with mocking intonation and tone of voice. When they do, they might just as well be using openly insulting words and epithets, because their body language makes their utterances unmistakably hostile.

The techniques in this book work superbly well when their intent is not contradicted by nonverbal messages, but they don't have the power to cancel the grammar of English. And the grammar of English has as a primary rule: *"When the words and the body language don't match, believe the body."*

WORKOUT SECTION

In this workout section I've given you a set of brief dialogues to analyze and revise in the same way that we've been working with the scenarios. Consider them carefully, looking for indications that a speaker:

- is failing to listen,
- is using Miller's-Law-in-Reverse,
- is making poor sensory mode or Satir Mode choices,
- is failing to use three-part messages where they're needed, or
- is simply guilty of clumsiness or poor strategy.

Then rewrite the dialogues to correct those errors. If you have trouble, I suggest that you record the dialogues and listen to them, and do the same with your proposed revisions. That usually clarifies things.

Dialogue One

Jeff: "What did you call me in about, Carla? Is there a problem?"

Carla: "There sure **is**! You **know** moonlighting is against company rules! I suppose you thought you could get **away** with it because you're the only **man** in this department, but you're **wrong**! Rule are RULES!"

Jeff: "I hear you."

Carla: "I should hope you **do**! And I expect you to live up to your **commit**ment here and quit that second job **immediate**ly!"

Jeff: "Like I said—I hear you."

Carla: "And what is THAT supposed to mean?!"

Jeff: "It means you and your company can take this job and stuff it."

Carla: "But Jeff, **wait** a minute! Don't be so **touchy,** for heavens sake! I'm sure we can work this **out!**"

Jeff: "No we can't, Carla. So long!" [Walks out.]

Dialogue Two

Doctor: "Mr. Jonson, I've got some bad news for you."

Patient: "I see. . . . What is it, Doctor?"

Doctor: "You've got cancer. And because of the tumor's location, I'm putting you down for immediate surgery. Go straight to the hospital—you can get your wife to bring you anything you need from home."

Patient: [Voice shaking.] "But **wait** a minute! I—"

Doctor: "Sorry, Mr. Jonson; I know it's rough. The nurse out front will give you the papers." [Leaves the room.]

Dialogue Three

Prof: "Ann, I'm sorry—you failed your exam."

Ann: "NO! That's NOT POSSible! I worked so HARD!"

Prof: "I know you did, but—"

Ann: "NOW what am I going to do???"

Prof: "You'll have to repeat the course, but—"

Ann: "I CAN'T do the course over! I can't get another student LOAN! And I—"

Prof: "**Listen,** Ann—I don't want to sound harsh, but hysterics won't **help.** When you're ready to talk like an adult, call me. I'll be happy to discuss this with you."

Ann: "Oh, **I** get it! It's OKAY to kick ME around, because I'm just a PART-time student! If I was one of your—"

Prof: [Icily.] "I have nothing more to say to you, Ann. Excuse me." [Leaves the room.]

Dialogue Four

Andy: "Hey, Nancy, why the long face? I thought you'd be **glad** I'm quitting that dead-end job I'm in and starting my own business!"

Nancy: "But that **marketing** company you're joining is just a **scam**, Andy! You're **making** a terrible mis**take**!"

Andy: "You know, Nancy, women have **no** stomach for taking risks; they're **rotten** judges of business potential! But I **thank** you for your con**cern**—of **course**."

Nancy: [Sighs.] "**All** right, Andy; you're a **grown** man. Whatever **you** want to do Is **okay** with me."

Dialogue Five

Rose: "I thought you'd be as excited about this as I am, Gordon. Why are you **frowning** at me like that?"

Gordon: "HONestly, Mother! You know what will happen to the money you give that outfit? It'll help pay fat salaries to a bunch of greedy BUREAUcrats, THAT'S what!"

Rose: "You young people always think your parents have no sense, Gordon—I'm used to that. And I'm not going to let it stand in my way, not when children are going hungry and I could help."

Gordon: "ALL RIGHT, Mother! It's YOUR MONey! You go right ahead and throw it away if you WANT to!"

Dialogue Six

John: "Your strategy would probably work, Lee; it's clever. But from a **Christian** point of view, it's WAY out of line! **First** of all, you—"

Lee: "**Don't start**, John! Just CUT it out!"

John: "**There's no** reason for you to take that tone with me! Who do you think you **are**, anyway?"

Lee: "I'm your **friend**! But I'm **not** going to listen to all that **religious** claptrap, so don't **start!**"

John: "You'll be **sorry** you didn't listen when you find yourself in JAIL, buddy!"

Dialogue Seven

Wes: "Listen, I was worried about that talk, but I think it turned out okay! I don't mind telling you, all that clapping was music to my ears!"

Bill: "Uh-huh."

Wes: "Well, come on . . . tell me what **you** thought!"

Bill: "Well, the way I look at it, if you give a speech you're obligated to see to it that your **facts** are right!"

Wes: [Coldly.] "So I made a couple of mistakes."

Bill: "Hey, you **asked** for my opinion, you know!"

Wes: "If you thought the mistakes were such a big **deal**, why didn't you speak up **then**?"

Bill: "I **should** have, but—"

Wes: "But you were **too chicken, weren**'t you? Just like you're too chicken to make a speech your**self**, so all **you** do is nitpick **other** people's speeches!"

Nothing is more frustrating than coming away from an interaction that went badly and having no idea why it went wrong. The temptation in such cases is always to decide that only one possible explanation exists: It happened because one of the people involved—perhaps yourself—is ignorant, or has a flawed character, or has unsavory motives, or worse. This shouldn't happen to you, now that you've been keeping records of your problem encounters in your Conflict Journal. You will be able to go back to them and analyze them just as we've been doing in this book; you'll then understand what went wrong and why and will know how to avoid such events in the future.

THOUGHT BITES

1. "Trying to force a lock bends the key, for which reason a truly intelligent man never forces an issue" (Watts, *Does It Matter?* 1971, 77).

2. "It is true . . . that Christian tradition is associated with 'mysteries' . . . but there is nothing mysterious about the command to love God above all things and to love our neighbor with the same love as we love ourselves. This twofold imperative, according to Christianity's founder, makes up the sum total of religion" (Graham, *End of Religion,* 1971, 20).

CHAPTER SEVEN

DELIVERING BAD NEWS AT HOME

> Do not answer a fool according to his folly,
> Lest you also be like him.
>
> **Proverbs 26:4**

When we find ourselves obliged to give negative messages to strangers, to associates we see only rarely—to anyone we have no close relationship with—we find it distasteful. When we have to fill that same role with someone very *close* to us, it's much worse, and distaste is no longer a strong enough word for our emotion.

SCENARIO SEVEN

"What's the matter, son? You've hardly touched your food—are you **sick**? Is there some problem with your **grades**?"

Jason stared down at his plate, trying to think what to say. He'd meant to get through this meal before making his announcement; they were supposed to be celebrating his upcoming graduation.

But it obviously wasn't going to work. "No!" he said quickly. "No, I'm fine! And my grades are all fine!"

He knew by the silence that they were waiting for him to go on; he swallowed hard, took a deep breath, and just blurted it out.

"Mom ... Dad ... I know this is really going to upset you, but I've got to tell you: I won't be coming to work with you at the *Courier*. I'm sorry; I just can't **do** it!"

"Jason!" Melanie Jones's voice was shrill. "You can't **mean** that!"

"I can't do it, Mom," Jason said again. "I'm really sorry ... I've accepted an offer from the *Potomac Politician* in Washington, D.C., starting Monday after graduation. It's not a **great** job, but I'm going to be a political journalist—it's a start."

Sam Jones had been staring at his son, obviously stunned, gripping his knife and fork more and more tightly as Jason talked. He laid both down carefully now and crossed his arms over his chest.

"SO!" he said. "You've played along with us all these years, while we scraped and saved and worked like dogs to come up with your tuition, but now that you've got your hands on your diploma you can drop the **act**! RIGHT?"

"No, Dad," Jason said miserably. "That's **not** right! And it's not fair. I wasn't acting, I really did think I'd want to work with you and Mom. The *Vendon Courier* has been in our family for almost a hundred years—that **means** something. But during this past year I've come to realize that it's just not right for **me**."

His mother started crying. "Jason, please, PLEASE. . . . You KNOW how much we've COUNTed on you to—" she began; but Sam Jones cut her off.

"Let **me** handle this, Melanie!" he snapped. "Jason, we had an agreement! We'd put you through school to get your journalism degree, you'd join us at the *Courier* when you graduated, and you'd take over when we retire. Remember? That was the

deal! Your mother and I have done **our** part—it hasn't been easy, but we've **done** it! Now it's time for you to do *YOURS*!"

This was turning out exactly the way Jason had expected; that certainty was the reason he'd put it off until the last possible minute, even though he knew it wasn't fair to his parents. His voice was unsteady as he answered his father.

"Dad, if you REALLY cared about me, you wouldn't WANT me to stay here and bury myself on a paper that hasn't printed any REAL news in fifty YEARS! If you'll just give me a chance to explain to you what I—"

"What do you MEAN, the *Courier* hasn't printed any real news in fifty years?!" Sam was beet-red with anger. "Listen, just because we don't fill up every page with murders and rapes and FILTH, that doesn't mean you'd be BURYing yourself! We put out a GOOD paper, we always HAVE, and if you had ANY brains at ALL you'd know how lucky you are to have a CHANCE to work there!"

"I DO have brains!" Jason insisted. "That's the PROBlem! If I didn't, I wouldn't MIND staying here! But—"

"Oh, Jason," his mother wailed, "I can't beLIEVE you would do this to us, after all we've done for you! How can you TREAT us like this? EVen a child like YOU ought to be able to under-stand—"

"I'm not a CHILD, Mother!" Jason shouted. "I'm a grown MAN! WHY can't either of you understand THAT? I'm an ADULT, and I have plans of my OWN!"

"Oh, YEAH?" his father shot back at him. "If you were an ADULT, you'd have paid your OWN way through college! Grown MEN don't have to depend on other people to SUPPORT them, Buster, and grown MEN keep their WORD!"

It went on and on. The things they said to each other were going to be hard to forget, much less forgive. Jason had known it would be bad, and he knew he had it coming, if only because he'd let his parents go on all this time thinking he shared their plans. But he hadn't expected it to be *this* bad! In the end, just before he tore out of the house and slammed the front door behind him, he was horrified to hear himself yelling, "You two can't lock ME up for life on your stupid little paper! I'll pay you BACK your cursed money—that's all you REALLY care about ANYway!"

It wasn't true, and he knew it wasn't—and the *Courier* wasn't "a stupid little paper" either. *What's the matter with me, saying things like that?* he thought as he headed for the curb. *I could cut my tongue out!*

WHAT'S GOING ON HERE?

This scene is the kind of classic row that stage melodramas are made of, but the pain is absolutely real and down to earth. Whenever the people involved in such a breakdown are close, and the message is "I know I said I would, I know I promised you, but I've changed my mind," communication breakdown is probable. The more love there is, the more the unexpected change will feel like a bitter blow, and the more likely it is that the person responsible will make a bad situation worse by handling the announcement of the change abominably, as Jason has.

POINTS OF VIEW

Sam and Melanie have a quite clear perception of this situation. They've worked and sacrificed for years to get their only child the training he needs, so that he can join them in the family business and eventually take it over. They thought he was looking forward to carrying on the tradition just as they were. And now, out of the blue, he has turned on them and made everything they've done worthless. That Jason would throw away the family's proud heritage, that he could even consider letting the

Courier be taken over by strangers, that he places so little value on what matters so much to them, seems to Sam and Melanie to be the ultimate selfish betrayal. They are so deeply hurt and so shocked, they can't think clearly.

Jason doesn't see things that way, of course. He is an ambitious young man with a lot of talent and drive, and the last thing he wants to do is spend his life stuck on a small-town paper in the middle of nowhere. He has big plans—he sees himself becoming a top investigative reporter, uncovering the wicked deeds of the country's politicians, maybe getting a Pulitzer someday. It seems to him that his parents should be proud that he's willing to reach higher than the *Vendon Courier* and should support him in what he plans to do; it's not as if the *Courier* were the *New York Times*! It seems to him that their willingness to sacrifice his happiness, just to maintain a family myth, is stubborn and selfish, and that the "after all we've done for you" line can only be called *blackmail*. How could they put him in a position like that, back him up against the *wall* like that? Like Sam and Melanie, he is too hurt and too angry to think clearly.

There's right on both sides in this argument, and plenty of blame to go around. The question of whether the Joneses are morally right to expect their young son to live up to the deal he made—or should let that go and wish him well—is best left to the specialists in ethics and theology, along with whether it's Jason's moral obligation to sacrifice his own happiness for his parents. "Honor your father and mother," the Bible says, but does honor have to mean total sacrifice? We'll set those questions aside here and concentrate on the situation at hand. Clearly, Jason isn't willing to be a martyr. Are there things he could have done to break the bad news to his parents without creating such wreckage in all their lives? Assuming that his parents aren't willing to be martyrs either, are there things they could have done so that their response to the news would be less likely to tear the family apart?

Yes, there are, I'm glad to say. This is very important. Because it often happens that when something like this is over and a few months have gone by, those involved realize that it wasn't the end of the world after all—*but the terrible things that were said at the time, in the heat of the moment, continue to stand as a formidable barrier to reconciliation.*

A COMMUNICATION TECHNIQUE: MANAGING THE ENGLISH VERBAL ATTACK PATTERNS, PART ONE

Have you ever thought about the extraordinary *ease* with which we're able to construct utterances that hurt other people? We don't have to struggle at all, we don't have to plan; the verbal slaps just come flying off our tongues. Even those of us who would never turn on others with open curses and slurs and epithets have no trouble producing one hurtful utterance after another. *Why?*

The question is easily answered: Whatever gets most of our attention and effort is what will thrive. *Anything you feed will grow.* We have put so much of our resources into causing pain with language that our grammar has come to have an inventory of special patterns reserved specifically for that purpose, and we practice those patterns with deadly regularity and apparent enthusiasm. I call them the *English verbal attack patterns*—VAPs, for short. Here are a handful of typical examples:

- "If you really CARED about your health, YOU wouldn't spend all your time lying around watching TELEvision!"
- "WHY don't you ever think about ANYbody but yourSELF?"

- "You could at LEAST TRY to get to work on time!"
- "EVen a person YOUR age ought to know SOMEthing about music!"
- "You're not the ONly person with PROBlems, you know!"
- "Don't you even CARE if you're BREAKing your mother's HEART?"
- "SOME people would really RESENT it if they came home to a PIGsty every day!"

Do they sound familiar? Of course they do! We begin using these patterns as soon as we can talk, and we go on with them till we die. They are as nearly *automatic* in our speech as answering "Thank you" with "You're welcome." You will have noticed that all of them contain extra emphasis on words and parts of words, and that all but one include lots of very personal vocabulary—two of the defining characteristics of hostile English. And the final example is not a true exception. The person who hears it will know, from the tune the words are set to, that it's just a Computer Mode variation on "WHY do I have to come home every day to a HOUSE that looks like a PIGsty? Don't you EVer CLEAN?"

RECOGNIZING THE ENGLISH VERBAL ATTACK PATTERNS

You recognize the attack patterns automatically, the way you recognize a sentence as a question or a promise or a threat, the way you recognize the vocabulary of a sensory system. It's internalized knowledge. For clarity's sake, however, and in order to set up an efficient index for the information in your long-term memory, we need to describe the VAPs as clearly as possible. Every VAP is hostile language, but not every item of hostile lan-

guage is an example of a VAP. We know the VAPs by four characteristics.

1. They always have two parts: an open and obvious attack
   (called the *bait* because it's the part intended to get the listener's attention) and at least one other attack that is sheltered in a presupposition. Sometimes the two parts are
   clearly separated; sometimes they are mingled together in
   complicated ways.

A presupposition is a chunk of meaning that a native speaker
of a language understands even when it isn't "there" in the words.
For example, "Even **John** could pass **this** class!" presupposes
that John's a pathetically poor student and that the class is trivially easy. Neither of those propositions appears in the words of
the sentence. Looking up all those words in the dictionary
wouldn't tell you that either John or the class is flawed in any
way. Nevertheless, if you speak English fluently you know that
those two ideas are included, and the *reason* you know is because
they are presuppositions of the sentence. Look at the following
example:

- "If you REALLY loved me, you wouldn't always try to make
  me look STUPID in front of our FRIENDS!"

This pattern, which children learn very early, is one in which
the two parts are clearly separated. The bait is open and obvious: "You always try to make me look stupid in front of our
friends." The other attack, "You don't love me," is a presupposition of "If you REALLY loved me"; that's what "If you REALLY
loved me" means. The most important parts of the pattern are
its basic structure and the tune, of course, not the exact words,

so that this same attack may have a variety of slightly different versions. Here are a few of the many possibilities:

- "If you really LOVED me, YOU wouldn't always try to make me look STUPID in front of our FRIENDS!"
- "If you LOVED me, YOU wouldn't always try to make me look STUPID in front of our FRIENDS!"
- "If you really CARED for me, you wouldn't always try to make me look DUMB in front of our FRIENDS!"

If you had to memorize all the possible forms this example could take, you'd be in deep trouble; it would in fact be impossible. But you don't. In your internal grammar you have this *pattern*, with all the rules that are needed for recognizing it when you hear it and fitting words and intonation into it when you use it yourself. Once I've called it to your attention, you will recognize any example of this particular VAP that comes your way, including the Computer Mode-ish versions like this one:

- "Someone who really LOVES his wife [*her husband*] wouldn't always try to make her [*him*] look STUPID in front of their FRIENDS!"

2. Like all hostile English, the VAPs contain much personal language and many extra emphatic stresses on words and parts of words.

Another VAP that people learn in very early childhood is the pattern that starts with a heavily stressed "WHY" followed by "do [*or are*] you ALways" or "don't [*aren't*] you EVer." It's an instructive pattern, because it demonstrates so clearly that the attack is in the tune rather than the words. Look at these sentences:

- "Why don't you ever type your homework?"
- "WHY don't you ever TYPE your HOMEwork?!"

The first question is just that, a question; the person asking it has noticed that you always turn in handwritten homework and is curious about it. Although the second example contains exactly the same words, it has a different meaning and is an attack. Both sentences have as a presupposition "You never type your homework." Both have the presuppositions that go with all English questions: "I have reason to believe that you have the item of information I'm asking about" and "I have the right to ask you to share it with me." But example (b) has one *more* presupposition, carried by the extra stress on that "WHY": "Whatever your answer is, I'm telling you in advance, it's not good enough!" That presupposition is the sheltered attack. The fact that all those presupposed words are carried by nothing but the extra stress on "why" is amazing, but it's true.

As with the "If you REALLY . . ." pattern, this one can occur with many variations in its exact wording; what makes it an attack is its basic form and its tune.

3. VAPs ordinarily have a neutral "twin"—another sentence that contains exactly the same words, but is *not* an attack.

We've already seen this illustrated in the "WHY/Why" pair of examples we just examined.

4. People who use a VAP ordinarily have little or no interest in the answer. If they were expressing its neutral twin, they *would* be interested.

For example, someone who asks you "Why do you eat so much junk food?" may be rude and tactless, but that person is genuinely interested in hearing you answer the question; it's not an attack. But the person who asks you, "WHY do you eat SO MUCH JUNK food??!" couldn't care less why you eat so much junk food; it's an attack, and what is wanted is not an answer but a *fight*.

We don't need to look at all the English VAPs here. (I think there probably are no more than about twenty of them, but every once in a while I come across a new one, so I can't be positive.) Now that we've set up an index for that part of your internal grammar, you'll know them when you hear them. We'll look at just one more, one that has the bait and the sheltered attack mixed up together instead of neatly separated. It looks like this:

"EVen a MAN should be able to fix BREAKfast!"

Notice that you do know what that means; it should give you a profound respect for your miraculous human mind that you do. If you had to list the various things it means, these five sequences —which are curiously intermingled in the example and impossible to separate out—would appear on your list:

1. There's something wrong with being a man.
2. There's something wrong with being unable to fix breakfast.
3. Breakfast is trivially easy to fix.
4. You're a man.
5. You can't fix breakfast.

This pattern is so powerful that it can get along without the opening "even," as in "A MAN should be able to fix BREAKfast!" and "A WOMAN should be able to change a TIRE!" When someone says those sentences to you, you *hear* the "even" even (there's that word again!) though it's not "there."

RESPONDING TO ENGLISH VERBAL ATTACK PATTERNS

The most important thing to know about the VAPs is that they are *action chains*. The chain has a set of parts in a fixed order; if it's interrupted at any point, it fails. Here's the script for the chain; this is what the verbal attacker expects, and wants, to happen:

- The attacker throws out the VAP sequence.
- The targeted victim takes the bait and runs with it, responding to it directly in hostile language.
- There is a volley of attacks and counterattacks, until one of the speakers gives up and stops participating.

Because this is how things are, you want to be certain that you never let a VAP attack succeed. It can't happen without the participation of the intended victim; there has to be someone present to feed the attacker the next line in the script. To understand how this works, we're going to look at two versions of a dialogue. In the first one, the attack succeeds; in the second, it fails. Watch carefully.

WHEN THE ATTACK SUCCEEDS

Tim: "WHY do you ALWAYS eat SO MUCH JUNK food??!"

Joe: "What do you MEAN? I do NOT eat a lot of junk food!"

Tim: "Oh, YEAH? What about that TWINKIE I saw you eating at noon? You call that HEALTHY?"

Joe: "Hey, I didn't have time to go to LUNCH today! I just ate what I could GRAB!"

Tim: "Well, what about that PIZZA I saw you eating in the HALL yesterday? You were—"

Joe: "WAIT a minute! Just WHO DO YOU THINK YOU ARE, spying on me all the time, ANYway?"

Tim: "SPYING on you? Wow, you not only live on TWINKIES

and PIZza, Buddy, you're PARAnoid, TOO!"

Joe: "LISTEN, I've had ALL I'm going to TAKE from you!"

WHEN THE ATTACK FAILS

Tim: "WHY do you ALWAYS eat SO MUCH JUNK food??!"

Joe: "I think it's because of something that happened to me when I was just a little kid. We were living in Detroit at the time. . . . No. Wait. It couldn't have been Detroit, because that was the year my Aunt Grace came to see us and brought her dog. I guess we must have been living in St. Louis then. Anyway—"

Tim: "Hey. Joe. Never mind, okay?"

Joe: "Whatever you say."

You see how this works? When Joe takes the bait and hits back, he is giving Tim exactly what Tim wants—the long VAP session of heated attacks and counterattacks. He does that by responding directly to the bait, the accusation that he eats way too much junk food. *This rewards Tim for the attack and trains him to be an even better verbal abuser.* When the attack fails, Joe responds instead to the presupposition that Tim wants the information requested, and does so in excruciatingly tedious detail. This move (called *The Boring Baroque Response*) is gentle and nonabusive, but it makes it impossible for Tim to go on with the attack; it is an excellent example of turning the other cheek. It interrupts the action chain and the hostility loop that Tim was trying to set up, and the attack fails. Tim can start another attack, if he's determined to "get" Joe, but *this* one is over.

Here are the rules for responding to VAPs:

Rule One:

Ignore the bait, no matter how tempting.

Rule Two:
Respond, with neutral body language, to some other presupposed part of the utterance.

Here's another example:

Ann: "If you REALLY wanted to get ahead in this department, you wouldn't come in LATE every day!"

Sue: "Of course I want to get ahead in the department; it's very important to me."

or

"When did you start thinking I don't want to get ahead in the department?"

The bait in the example is "You come in late every day." Sue has ignored that, interrupting the action chain, and responded—neutrally, without any hitting back—to the presupposed "you don't want to get ahead in the department." When she does that, the attack fails.

Whether you answer an attack with "When did you start thinking. . . ." (the most neutral question you could ask, and entirely nonconfrontational) or with the "Of course" response, depends on whether you want to listen to the answer to the "when" question. If not, make the other choice.

You can also respond to an "If you REALLY . . ." (or any other) VAP with a Boring Baroque Response. If Sue had done that, it could have gone something like this:

"Hearing you say that reminds me of an article about the problem of lateness in the workplace that I read in the *Wall Street Journal* only the other day! No—wait a minute. It couldn't have been the *Wall Street Journal*, it must have been the *New York Times*, because we were so busy last week that I didn't even get a chance to read the *Journal*. And I was sorry about that, because it's one of the most useful sources for information about research on workplace problems. In fact, I think it's *better* than the *Times*, although many people would probably disagree with me. Anyway, I..."

When radio and television stations bring ex-criminals on the air for advice about protecting oneself from crime and ask them how they choose someone to mug, the answer can always be summed up as "I look for somebody who's muggable." The same thing is true of *verbal* attackers. When you answer their attack with a Boring Baroque Response, the message you give them is that you're not verbally "muggable," you're no fun at all as a VAP-ping partner, you're not going to reward them for attacking you, and it's a waste of their time to try that with you. That's an excellent outcome. It doesn't require you to either hit back or grovel, and there's no loss of face on either side of the interaction.

Again, you choose between Boring Baroque and the other alternatives on the basis of the circumstances in which the attack happens. Do you want to cut off the interaction sharply and see the attacker just move on? Then the Boring Baroque Response is a good choice.

Do you want to stop the attack but continue the interaction? Then choose a "When did you start thinking. . . ." question.

The "Of course . . ." response falls in between. It doesn't ask for more input the way a question does; on the other hand, it doesn't make the attacker feel motivated to go away. And you'd never want to use a Boring Baroque Response with someone whose attack was motivated by fear or pain or some other extenuating circumstance. When a terrified family member says to a nurse, "If you REALLY wanted to help my mother, YOU wouldn't just let her lie there SUFFERING and do NOTHING FOR her!" it would be totally inappropriate to launch into "I think it's because of something . . ." that happened to you or that you read. Common sense, and your internal grammar, will make your choice among the possible responses clear; trust them. Just *don't take the bait*.

Always, when I present this technique in seminars, people object that ignoring verbal attackers' bait is "letting them get **away** with it!" That's a misunderstanding. When you take the bait and give an answer that will be something the attacker has no real interest in, you provide the attacker with exactly what he or she wants by participating in an undignified verbal slapfest; *that* is "letting them get away with it"! It should not ever happen. Because every time you do it, you reinforce the verbal abuser's conviction that you're a "muggable" victim who can be relied upon to provide VAPping services on demand, as well as reinforcing the idea that verbal violence is an acceptable form of communication.

ANOTHER LOOK
AT SCENARIO SEVEN

We would all agree that Jason Jones's gravest error was putting off telling his parents his decision until the very last possible moment; that's rarely a wise move. We know *why* he did that, of course. He was certain that no matter *when* he made the announcement, the result would be a horrendous family fight. This is no excuse, but it's instructive. We're deeply shocked when we learn that we have in our circle someone whose spouse has suddenly demanded a divorce (or has come home to find the spouse simply gone), someone whose child has suddenly run away or been arrested or joined the growing bitter harvest of teenage suicides—all "without any warning." Whenever we hear people say that someone in their immediate family has done some dreadful thing "without warning," we can be reasonably sure that communication had broken down in that family long before the event. The problem in Scenario Seven is less tragic, but it's the same sort of difficulty.

Let's assume that the situation is as shown, that Jason postpones his announcement till the last minute and makes it—clumsily and hastily—during the family dinner intended to celebrate his graduation. This is a serious error on his part, but there it is. It will be obvious to you that many things about the language in the scenario need to be changed, but suppose we focus in this chapter only on the verbal attack patterns: With that narrower focus, what could have been done to make the occasion less horrific? There are five examples of verbal attack patterns in the dialogue:

1. Jason: "If you REALLY cared about me, you wouldn't WANT me to stay here and bury myself on a paper that hasn't printed any REAL news in fifty YEARS!"

2. Sam: "If you had ANY brains at ALL, you'd know how lucky you are to have a CHANCE to work there!"

3. Melanie: "EVen a child like YOU ought to be able to understand [*that you have to live up to your promises and do your duty, etc.*] . . ."

4. Jason: "WHY can't either of you understand THAT [*that I'm not a CHILD,etc.*]?"

5. Sam: "If you were an ADULT, you'd have paid your OWN way through college!"

This is how a VAP session is *supposed* to go; all these people are following the standard script with passion and skill. Jason throws out the opening attack; Sam takes the bait and runs with it; a volley of attacks and counterattacks follows, with Melanie joining the fray, until Jason finally gives up and flees the scene. His opening was spectacularly hurtful; it contains two direct chunks of bait plus one sheltered attack:

- *Bait:* "Your newspaper hasn't published any real news for fifty years."
- *Bait:* "You want me to stay here and work on your newspaper even though that would be like burying myself."
- *Sheltered Attack:* "You don't really love me."

Jason knows quite well that his father and mother treasure the family newspaper and look upon it as a shining legacy. Most such papers dwindle away quickly; that theirs has survived for almost a century is impressive. For Jason to attack that newspaper viciously, twice in one utterance, is just about as low as he could stoop. And since it is his father who *writes* most of the paper, Jason can't attack it without attacking Sam personally at the same time. He might just as well have hit his father over the head with a club; it would have been no more shocking and no more painful than his language, especially after all that Sam and Melanie have done for him in this context.

It is natural for Sam to feel that his son has struck him, and Melanie as well. At this point, Sam faces the demand that he turn the other cheek in response to this injury. For him to remain detached would be difficult, given all the hostile language that has already been exchanged *before* the VAP was flung at him. But he has the wisdom of maturity and experience; he can do it.

Jason has just said, "If you REALLY cared about me, you wouldn't WANT me to stay here and bury myself on a paper that hasn't printed any REAL news in fifty YEARS!"

Sam's goal is to respond in such a way that Jason's attack fails and the hostilities end, so this important matter can be discussed rationally and carefully. Fighting about it will only make his son more convinced that staying is a mistake, thus closing off all possibility of compromise, which is not in the best interests of *anyone* in the family. Sam's best strategy—for everyone involved, not just for Jason—is to ignore the insults to himself and the newspaper, respond directly to the sheltered attack, and then wait for Jason's next move. A probable result:

Sam: "Of course I care about you, Jason. When did you start thinking I don't?"

Jason: "Dad, I don't really think that . . . I don't know why I said that."

Sam: "When young people feel guilty, they tend to say things in haste—things they don't really mean."
[Computer Mode]

or

"Nothing is harder than speaking carefully and rationally through a fog of *guilt;* young people in that situation say things they don't mean."
[Computer Mode]

or

"I hear you, Jason. I hear *guilt* talking, and I'm positive that you don't mean the things you just said."

Jason: "I can't help feeling guilty, Dad—but I *do* mean it when I say I can't stay and work here."

Sam: "Let's talk about that, Son. Your mother and I would

like to hear about the plans you've made, and we very much want to know why you feel that the *Courier* can't be part of those plans."

Once this exchange has taken place, there's no reason why the other four VAPs should ever be spoken: All of them were responses—counterproductive, hostility-feeding responses—to Jason's opening. In the original scenario, where Sam took the bait, a fight was the only probable outcome; when he refrains from doing that, he adds discussion and negotiation to the options.

Sam and Melanie may still be unable to change Jason's mind, of course. But avoiding the terrible *fight* over the issue has three positive effects. First, it increases their chances of persuading him. Second, it increases the chance that even if Jason does go off to Washington, D.C., he may in a year or two be willing to come back to the family paper, with additional, and valuable, experience under his belt. Third, and most important, it preserves the unity of the family.

A set of vicious verbal blows, given and returned, would stand as a major barrier to all three of those positive effects. That's a very high price to pay for the short-lived satisfaction Sam and Melanie might have gained from hitting back at Jason and participating in the fight.

WORKOUT SECTION

1. Set up a verbal attack patterns page in your Conflict Journal, so that you can record VAP data in your own language environment as part of your database.

Verbal Attack Pattern
Incident Log
Date and Time:

The situation:

The VAP that [name] threw out:

What was said in reply:

What was said next: [repeat line as many times as needed]

How it all turned out:

What might have been done differently:

What I learned from this interaction:

---

2. Go back to Scenario Seven and analyze it for problems other than the VAPs. Identify the sensory modes and Satir Modes being used and problems they may have caused. Look for places where people stop listening or fail to use Miller's Law, as well as points at which a three-part message might have been useful.

3. Here is a set of VAPs for you to work with; some have one VAP tucked away inside another. For each one, identify the bait and the sheltered attack(s) as shown in the example.

- "If you were a REAL doctor, YOU wouldn't NEGLECT your patients the way you do!"
  Bait: "You neglect your patients."
  Sheltered Attack: "You're not a real doctor."

- "If you have any morals at ALL, you'll STOP spending all your spare time with your WORTHless FRIENDS!"
- "WHY don't you EVer think about ANYbody's NEEDS but your OWN?"
- "If you REALLY wanted me to get good grades, YOU'D buy me a comPUTer like all the OTHER kids have got!"
- "EVEN a reCEPtionist could have closed THAT deal!"
- "A first-year GRAD student would know that EVen professors with TENure have to publish SOMEthing!"

- "WHY do you spend your WHOLE day watching TELEvision?? If you really MEANT it when you say you're trying to find a job, you wouldn't just SIT there the whole day long!"
- "If you were REALLY a Christian, YOU'D at least TRY to do something to help the poor!"
- "EVen a LAWyer ought to have SOME sense of ethics!"

4. In this chapter I mentioned that it's not appropriate to use the Boring Baroque response to an attack that is due to someone's panic, exhaustion, or anything of that kind. For the "WHY . . ." attack, the alternative is often to ignore the bait and respond to the presupposition that whatever you're accused of ALWAYS happens, without exception, by making that false on the spot. For example, to a panicked child's "WHY don't you ever LISTEN to me when I try to TELL you what's WRONG??!", you could say, "Tell me the one thing that's bothering you most this very minute"—and then *listen*. (If you truly cannot do that, you can say, "I have to leave now, and there's no way I can postpone that. But I'll be back at noon, and when I get here I want you to come tell me the one thing that's bothering you most right that minute. Agreed?") I recommend setting up a *separate* page for incidents like these in your Conflict Journal.

5. Read the article by Nancy Gibbs in *Time* titled, "The EQ Factor" (1995, 60–68). Its subtitle says that "New brain research suggests that emotions, not IQ, may be the true measure of human intelligence." (Ask your librarian to find it for you if the 1995 issues aren't on your library shelves, or find it on the Internet.) The article is a good summary of Daniel Goleman's research on emotional intelligence; it will give you more insight into why communications skills are so critically important and why their absence can be such a severe handicap.

Thought Bites

1. "When He said, 'Be perfect,' He meant it. . . . It is hard; but the sort of compromise we are all hankering after is harder—in fact, it is impossible. It may be hard for an egg to turn into a bird; it would be a jolly sight harder for it to learn to fly while remaining an egg" (Lewis, *Inspirational Writings,* 1987, 296).

2. "We often poison and wound each other, especially our children, with words. You may have grown up with parents who used words as weapons, and hoped you wouldn't do the same with your children. But you will probably repeat the behavior unless you break the pattern and develop healthy communication . . . . Such a change is possible" (Wright, "Toxic Talk," 1991, 24).

3. "The human species thrives on violence and expresses it politically through tribal groups. Never is it fully under control, and we accept this as a fact of life. Indeed, we are barely able to control it in our own cities, which are coming increasingly to resemble the nightmare world of *A Clockwork Orange*" (Steel, "Let Them Sink" 1992, 15).

Do you agree with this assessment? Are we in fact justified in accepting the claim that we "thrive on violence"? What does the word "thrive" presuppose?

CHAPTER EIGHT

DEFUSING VERBAL COMBAT

Let every man be swift to hear, slow to speak, slow to wrath.

James 1:19

"Who *started* it?"

That question is of great importance in a court of law; many hours and many thousands of dollars may be devoted to answering it. And although we are said to be a Christian nation, *no* one in a court of law is ever going to say that the case must be thrown out because the person injured should have turned the other cheek. (If explicit evidence of the gap between our preaching and our practice is needed, this fact will serve nicely.)

In ordinary conflicts in daily life, however, matters are very different. As we've seen in previous chapters, *the decision for or against hitting back moves from person to person with each linguistic turn.*

Suppose I slap you verbally; now you have the choice of turning the other cheek, fleeing, groveling, or hitting me back. Suppose you choose to hit back; now *I* am the one who faces that choice. And so it goes, back and forth, until one of us "loses." It takes at least two of us to have that fight, with the roles of attacker and victim being chosen in regular alternation. Our society perceives assaults carried out in self-defense differently, but they are still assaults. And although it's usually easy—in the legal sense—to establish that Person X "started it" in a given altercation, assigning *ultimate* responsibility is often extremely difficult, if not impossible.

We don't know why people do physical hitting. We don't know why they start hitting on the vast scale that we call "war." Social scientists propose a variety of explanations, ranging from plain and simple human wickedness at one extreme to human helplessness—based on the idea that genetics makes physical violence part of the definition of humankind—at the other. We can say that a particular battle started *after* some event that angered or outraged others, but we cannot say why those who were angered or outraged chose physical force as their response. We know quite a lot more, however, about why people use *verbal* force.

There are five reasons. Sadism—a desire to cause pain and to find pleasure in that pain—is only one of the reasons, and it's the rarest. Sadism is mental illness and deformity of the spirit; you're unlikely to come across it twice in a lifetime. The *common* reasons are these four:

1. The attacker is suffering such intense exhaustion or fear or illness or other impairment that all control has been lost.
2. The attacker is trying to fill the normal need for human attention and knows no other way to do that except to verbally attack someone.
3. The attacker has a goal that makes the attack just, and is trying to achieve that goal, but is unaware that nonviolent measures for doing so exist.

4. The attacker has a goal that makes the attack just, and is trying to achieve that goal, without having first tried to find and to use nonviolent alternatives.

All of these reasons, once you understand that *they* are what lies behind the attack, will allow you to remain detached and rational. All four will allow you to consider the situation without feeling the negative emotions that lead to emotional hijackings and make conflict inevitable. In the hands of a sadist you are right to be afraid, and compassion for the attacker's illness may only be possible for the saintly; but again, sadism is *exceedingly* rare. It's important to understand this, because it has become our habit to immediately conclude that the verbal abuser's motivation *is* a desire to cause pain, and find pleasure in doing so, and that conclusion is seriously flawed.

Your feelings about the language in verbal attacks won't change when you understand the reasons behind it. You'll still find it offensive and unacceptable. But your response to *the person using the language* will be different. Dealing with someone you perceive as cruel and evil is very different from responding to someone you perceive as uninformed or lazy or panicked. Your reaction won't be, "This person is trying to HURT me—I have to DEFEND myself!" To reason 1 (the attacker is suffering intense exhaustion or fear or illness) it will be "Poor soul; is there anything I can do to help?" To reasons 2 and 3 (the attacker is trying to fill the need for human attention or achieve a goal but does not know how to accomplish it) it will be "Poor soul; this is the best he [she] can do." Even to reason 4, the one that reflects laziness and carelessness, your strongest reaction will be annoyance rather than fear or rage.

It may surprise you to know that a very large part of verbal abuse is due to the second reason: the desire for human attention. You know how a child who is normally well-behaved will suddenly do dreadful things when the parents are giving a large party and the child feels ignored and left out? That child, like a school-yard bully, would rather have *negative* attention than none at all. Many people today who grow up without ever learning basic social skills *have* learned that by verbally abusing others they can reliably get and hold attention, and they know no other way. Of course they would rather be liked and welcomed and praised, but they have no idea how to get those reactions. Like the child, they will settle for the attention that goes with arguments and fights, if they believe that's the only alternative to being ignored. This is especially sad, since their behavior makes people's negative reactions toward them even stronger. You should expect to observe a *lot* of hostile language that comes from this need for attention; you will find it easy to recognize.

Now let's look at an example of verbal combat that results from some of the other reasons on the list.

SCENARIO EIGHT

Clay grew more and more worried as he listened to what Charles Hanniver was saying in the sales meeting. His boss was carefully laying out an advertising strategy for his three agents to use. It sounded like something that would probably sell a lot of insurance. But it was obvious to Clay that the customers would never receive what they'd believe had been promised to them.

"Everybody understand? Any questions?" Charles asked finally.

The other two men nodded. "No questions, Charlie," Don Park said. "It's clear."

"I *do* have a question," Clay began. "The problem is that the way you worded the material makes it sound like the customer is getting a much better deal than is really the **case!**"

"Sure!" Charles said, grinning at him. "So?"

Clay was surprised. He'd expected to have trouble making his touchy boss admit that there *was* a deception, and he'd been braced for that. He'd survived more than a few of Hanniver's tantrums over the years, and he was used to them. But he'd never expected *this*.

"Clay," Charles went on, in the indulgent tone of voice people use with cranky toddlers, "I was **very** careful putting this together, and I've had our attorney look at it. There's not one word in this new sales pitch that could be used against us in court. We're **okay** on this!"

"But, Charlie," Clay protested, "you **can't** seriously be telling us that we're supposed to deliberately mislead our **cus**tomers!"

Charles set the file down and looked straight at Clay; all the indulgence was gone now. "Johnson," he snapped, "you could at least TRY to behave like a grown man! This is how the game is PLAYED! We're not in Sunday school, this is BUSIness! If you REALLY wanted to get ahead in this world, you wouldn't make me spend half my time exPLAINing things to you!"

"What do you MEAN, I make you spend half your time explaining things to me?" Clay demanded. He was outraged. "I've been in this business for almost twenty YEARS, Charlie, and you're WAY out of line saying that you—"

"OH? What about last Tuesday morning when you couldn't figure out how to set up that **Jacob**sen account, Buddy? Remember **that**?"

Clay did remember, and it was true. It had been a complicated policy, and he hadn't felt comfortable setting it up without some input from Charles. He opened his mouth to point out how unusual that had been, but he didn't get a chance.

"And how about that liability policy you put together for the soup people over in **Car**terton? Remember **that**? You had to call me at HOME to get THAT one straight! **Remember**?"

It went on and on, right in front of the other two agents. Every single time Clay had consulted the boss was dragged out and waved in his face; every attempt he made to explain that these were *rare* occasions and fully justified was drowned in ridicule and sarcasm. He couldn't seem to find any spot in the argument where he could say what he desperately *wanted* to say, which was: *Charlie, you're only DOing this because there's no WAY you can defend the orders you're giving! You're making ME look like a jerk because you know that what you're telling us to do is WRONG!* By the time it was over he was shaking with anger, but he was too worn out and too humiliated to struggle any longer. *If I had any guts, I'd quit, right here and now,* he thought, *but I've got a family to support.*

When Charles finally wound up with a sharp, "Well? Do you have *any other questions*?" all Clay could manage to do was shake his head in miserable silence.

"Good!" Charles slapped the table hard, obviously very pleased with himself. "Then let's get to work!"

WHAT'S GOING ON HERE?

The easy and obvious analysis here is that Charles Hanniver is a sadistic boss who reveled in making a fool of Clay in front of his colleagues, and that Clay Johnson is a weakling who—although he began by taking the bait and counterattacking—didn't have courage enough to defend either his moral principles or himself for very long. As for who started it, it was Charles who used the first really abusive language, certainly. But it was Clay who made the first—and the second—accusation.

POINTS OF VIEW

The way Clay sees matters, his boss has *no* moral ground to stand on. Charles has ordered his agents to deceive their customers; he's proud of the deception and eager both to justify it and to take credit for it. He has attacked Clay viciously and publicly, with *no* justification, to punish him for pointing out the error of his ways. And it's obvious that he enjoyed humiliating Clay that way and feels good about having done so. The sheer *wicked-ness* of the man astonishes Clay.

Clay isn't sorry that he objected to the deceptive language. He sees that as his Christian duty, and he would do it again. But he doesn't just despise the boss, he also despises him *self*, because he didn't stick to his guns, and because he let Charles not only win but wipe the battlefield with him. He's had disagreements with the other man before, but he has never felt so deeply shamed and hurt; he hopes he will be able to forgive, but he's sure he will never be able to *forget* this episode. And he still has to face the moral dilemma: Is he going to follow orders and mislead customers or refuse to do that and risk losing his job? It makes him almost sick to realize that nothing at all was gained by the fight with his boss, and that more conflict is inevitable.

Charles has a very different view of what went on here. He knows the language in the advertising copy is deceptive, but he also knows it's completely legal. With competition in the insurance business as fierce as it is, he feels that he has to use the same kind of advertising techniques everybody else is using. After all, he has a family to support and employees who need their jobs; he has to keep profits high enough to meet those obligations. He had hoped that all the agents would understand what was going on and let the matter go by without rocking the boat. For Clay Johnson, an experienced agent who surely ought to know better, to actually bring up the minor deception and *challenge* him on it, in front of everybody, strikes him as a deliberate attempt to make trouble and to make him look bad.

Charles knows he was rough on Clay, but he can't see that he had any other choice. Clay had him backed into a corner where he had to defend himself or be humiliated in front of his agents. Since he couldn't defend the deceptive language Clay had stupidly put under a spotlight, attacking the other man personally seemed to be the only defense option available. He's not sorry for his behavior. Like Clay, he feels that he only did what he had to do. After all, it was Clay who set things up so that one of them had to win and the other had to lose. For the *boss* to have been the loser would have been entirely unacceptable.

Unlike Clay, Charles feels that he did *well*; he's just sorry that the hostilities aren't over yet—because Clay will undoubtedly tackle him about this issue again—and sorry that the opening battle took place in public. He hopes Clay will have better sense the next time.

In order to understand fully what happened in Scenario Eight, we need to take time now to examine, carefully and in detail, one of our culture's most powerful and pervasive concepts: the doctrine of the just war. Without it, much that goes on in our communication seems almost impossible to explain. Let's clear up the confusion.

THE DOCTRINE OF THE JUST WAR

The disagreement between Clay and Charles in the scenario is a classic, though miniature, *war*. Both parties consider themselves to be in the right; both consider their cause just; both feel obligated to do their duty as well as they are able to do it. Both use the same weapon—hostile language—to carry out their battle plan.

Charles won and Clay lost, which means that in this case the war was won by the side that was in the wrong. This happens sometimes; it always means there'll have to be another war later.

When the bad guy wins, the hostilities are only on hold until the good guy can gather up enough resources to try again; it's the good guy's *duty* to try again. This is just the way the world is, and it's all as American as apple pie. No further discussion is required, because there's nothing else to say. Right?

But then what about the requirement that we must turn the other cheek? Where did it go? Who canceled it?

War, on any scale, has always been a problem for a Christian nation. Although horrendous amounts of killing go on in the Old Testament, it says flatly that we must not kill. And yet, whenever human beings face evil in the form of tyrants, war presents itself as a moral obligation.

Our solution to this problem has been the doctrine of the *just war*. We need to understand exactly what this means, because it is so widely misunderstood. It does NOT mean that killing in a just war is accepted as moral and right. Not at all. We must not let the medals awarded for being skilled and effective at such killing confuse us about that. It means that such killing is permitted—is not considered murder—*because it is only an unfortunate and unavoidable* side effect *of doing what is moral and right.* That is, the soldier's intent in combat is not to harm the enemy, which would be an evil goal, but to do a number of very good things: uphold justice, protect the innocent, defend home and country, and so on. That people on the other side of the conflict are hurt or killed in the process is something we deeply regret, but it *is not our intent,* and therefore we have done no wrong. Crucial to this solution, however, are two absolute requirements.

First is the requirement that violence be the *last resort,* always and without exception. Only that circumstance can make the harm unavoidable. By this standard, even the most just of all wars represents human failure in that we ought to have found a nonviolent solution, but it is not *wrong.*

We've lost track of this requirement today in our interactions with others. A just war has always been defined as what moral law allows after every other possible method for putting down evil has been tried and no nonviolent alternative remains open to us. When that principle is extended to the miniature wars in our daily lives, attacking rather than turning the other cheek is also failure, but is permitted in exactly the same circumstances. After we've done everything else we can possibly do to right the wrong, after we have failed in spite of our best efforts, we are permitted to do violence—and not until. The harm that we might do to others in that last-resort situation is then only the unfortunate and unavoidable side effect of our actions. It would not (and must not) be our intent. The way we now admire Rambos and Terminators is a misunderstanding; the harm they do isn't something to be proud of.

The problem in our daily lives right now is that we have allowed verbal violence to become the second or third resort, and far too often the first. We have decided that it's okay to hurt others with language in order to achieve some necessary good. This is in complete agreement with the doctrine of the just war, but we have forgotten all about the need to try every other possible method for achieving that good before we attack. Worse yet, we've done this for so long now that a generation has grown up largely unaware that any other methods *exist*. Our little children, not yet able to pronounce the Rs, learn to say "If you WEALLY wuvved me," followed by expertly chosen bait. This is where we have failed.

The problem is not that we lack the sublime wisdom always to find a nonviolent solution to conflict; that goes with being human rather than divine, and is understandable. It's that too much of the time we don't even bother to *look* for one. We've let the knowledge of those nonviolent solutions be lost to everybody except highly trained, professional negotiators, as if such communication were needed only for hostage-takings, peace settlements in wars of nations, and labor/management haggling. The communication techniques you are learning in this book are all examples of such nonviolent solutions.

The second requirement is that violence must be carried out with great reluctance and regret. That, too, has been allowed to fall away from our cultural consciousness, so that people who are on the attack today often feel pride and pleasure rather than regret. When I do seminars, there are always people present who tell me that no doubt the techniques I'm teaching will work, but "I get a kick out of getting people going, pushing their buttons, and you're taking all the *fun* out of it!" I tell them, "It's not supposed to be fun." On the contrary.

For the Christian, there's nothing ambiguous or mysterious about this matter, and we can sum it up as follows. Getting into arguments is part of being human; it's not wrong. *Enjoying* the arguments, actively seeking them out for the pleasure of arguing, *is* wrong. Failing to turn the other cheek when it truly cannot be avoided and the cause is just isn't wrong; *enjoying* it when that happens *is* wrong.

For those who are indifferent to religious and ethical issues, fortunately, I can still make my case on the evidence: In every aspect of human life, the use of hostile language can be proved to be counterproductive, dangerous, and wasteful of all our human resources. Even for people whose only concern is "What's in it for me?" the language environment that will guarantee *them* the highest payoff is one of harmony rather than conflict.

MANAGING THE ENGLISH
VERBAL ATTACK PATTERNS,
PART TWO

This brings us back at last to the English verbal attack patterns. They are implements of battle, nothing more, and suited *only* for linguistic combat. They have no other use. Getting rid of them won't remove all hostile language from the language environment, but it's a good first step. And because they are so widely and frequently used, avoiding their use—and making sure that when they come along they never work—is a very substantial improvement. What's needed in order to follow through and deal with the VAPs properly is not saintliness but *detachment,* so that we can react to them rationally.

Jesus, whipped and tormented, said not one word in His own defense. Crucified, suffering unspeakable torture, fully capable of calling down legions of angels to take up His cause, He said only, "Father, forgive them, for they know not what they do." This is Detachment with a capital D, far beyond human abilities, and it is the model held up for us. We lack divine wisdom and divine compassion, but all we require in order to react to hostile language with detachment is a clear understanding of what's actually happening when hostile language is used; I am confident that you now have that understanding.

When I present the information about the English VAPs, people understand it easily. (As they should; it comes from their internal grammar.) When I do my work properly, they hear what I say and think, *"I knew that!"* That is, they recognize it as knowledge they already had but were unable to use efficiently because they had no reliable access to it. And they have no problem following the explanation of the just war doctrine, although many tell me that the stipulations for last resort and regret come as a complete surprise to them. At this point, I'm always given two reasons why, despite being fully informed, they still can't follow the rules for managing VAPs.

One is a reason we took up in Chapter 7—the idea that you have to counterattack when someone goes after you with a VAP because not to do so is "letting them get away with it." Suppose you've been attacked with "If you REALLY cared about your health, YOU wouldn't just SIT all day long, you'd get out and EXercise!" The attacker has no interest in whether you exercise or not. The bait has been chosen not to get your response to the issue, but because the attacker has reason to believe that you won't be able to ignore it. People say to me, "I just couldn't let that one go by—it was SO vicious and SO mean!" Think, please: When you go fishing, do you use boring bait? Of *course* the bait will be vicious and mean, because the attacker has learned that such bait *works*. When you take it and run with it, you reinforce that idea. Letting whatever words are in the bait "go by" is trivial. Falling for the tactic, allowing it to sucker you into an undignified time-wasting fight that has no purpose, *that* is "letting them get away with it."

The second reason I hear may surprise you. It's "I just couldn't let it go by—I felt so *guilty*!" Consider the situation of a nurse who is routinely approached by a verbally abusive doctor, and who has routinely served her as a VAPping partner. Suppose that when the nurse stops providing that service, the doctor says something like this:

> "You know, no matter **how** hard my day had been, no matter **how** many problems I'd faced, even if I'd seen one of my patients go straight down**hill**, it used to be that I could come talk to you for a little while and I'd **feel** better! You were **really** a **help** to me. You know? I felt like I could go **on**! But now . . . I don't know . . . something's wrong. You've **changed**. I can't **count** on you any more! I don't know what I'm going to **do**. You know what I mean?"

The nurse this happened to told me that her reaction was, *"Oh, my gosh! If I don't go on being her verbal victim, the* patients *will suffer! And it will be* my fault!" And the next time the doctor threw a VAP at her, she grabbed it and ran with it for all she was worth.

You'll recognize this as a classic technique from the grammar of English verbal violence, called "How to Lay a Guilt Trip on Someone." It's stuffed with personal vocabulary and extra emphasis on words and parts of words. It can turn up anywhere. It's common between spouses and between parent and son or daughter, especially adult sons or daughters. Often, as in the example, it works very well.

What has to be understood and remembered is that hostile language is just as toxic, just as dangerous, for the attacker as it is for the targeted victim. Hostility is a major risk factor for every disease and disorder known, across the board. There is no reason to feel guilty about denying a chronic verbal abuser exposure to such language by refusing to play the role of verbal victim for him or her. It's not kind or nice or nurturing to do so, any more than it's kind or nice or nurturing to give an alcoholic a cocktail. If guilt lies anywhere, it lies in rewarding the attacker's dangerous behavior by making it possible, even easy, for it to continue.

Let's go back now and apply this information to Scenario Eight, to see how it could have been used to produce satisfactory communication and head off the destructive combat.

ANOTHER LOOK AT SCENARIO EIGHT

There are two critical spots in the scenario where things go wrong. The first doesn't involve verbal attack patterns, but it sets the stage for them:

Clay: "The problem is that the way you worded the material makes it sound like the customer is getting a much better deal than is really the **case**!"
and
"But you **can't** seriously be telling us that we're supposed to deliberately mislead our **cus**tomers!"

Clay is *morally* right here, no question about it. But both of his utterances are *strategically* wrong. He knows that his boss is touchy and temperamental; he's been involved in altercations with him in the past. The message he wants to get across to Charles Hanniver is, "I hear you saying that we agents are supposed to lie to the customers, which is morally wrong." But the way he constructs that message backs his boss into a corner and poses an unacceptable loss of face. If Clay actually had had no other alternative, he could at least have made certain that he said these things to Charles in *private;* if it's important to him that the other agents know how he feels about this, he could tell *them* in private. Nothing compels Clay to make the challenge public as he did. However, even if a public statement of his convictions couldn't be avoided, he could do better: He is morally right about the issue of lying to customers, but he is morally wrong to oppose it by using hostile language as a first resort.

Both of Clay's utterances are examples of mild Blaming because of their personal vocabulary and extra emphatic stresses. Let's make them less hostile and confrontational by rewriting them in Computer Mode. Instead of "the way you worded the material"—which is a direct criticism of Hanniver's behavior—Clay could say:

Clay: "The way the material has been worded . . ."

      or

      "The wording of the material . . ."

Instead of "You **can't** seriously be telling us that we're supposed to deliberately mislead our **cus**tomers!"—which is an open accusation—he could say:

Clay: "The suggestion that customers should be misled is a bit puzzling."

Both of Clay's original statements carried with them a hostile metamessage that we can summarize like this: "I know you're the BOSS—but you're WRONG, and I'm CHALLenging you!" If Clay's goal is in fact to try to take over the company and overthrow Charles, that could be necessary. But when his goal is only to persuade Charles not to go through with the planned deception, it's a foolish move. It guarantees that the metamessage in reply will be "Oh, you want to take me on in PUBlic, do you? All right, take THIS!" followed by a full attack. That is precisely what happened in the scenario, and it was predictable. It served no useful purpose.

The second critical spot in the scenario is the one where the boss throws a hostile barrage containing two VAPs (one of which we haven't discussed previously) at Clay:

1. "You could at least TRY to behave like a grown man!"
2. "If you REALLY wanted to get ahead in this world, you wouldn't make me spend half my time exPLAINING things to you!"

Now Clay knows he is under attack. He's been told that he not only doesn't meet the standards for adult male behavior, he doesn't even do the bare-bones minimum of *trying* to meet them. He's been told that he doesn't really want to get ahead in this world, and he's been accused of making Charles spend half his time explaining things—the way a little boy does.

Clay has been verbally slapped not once but several times. If he thinks Charles did this to shame and hurt him, he will tend to react with anger or fear or both, and will almost certainly hit back;

this is what happens in the scenario. Clay steps right into the trap with, "What do you MEAN, I make you spend half your time explaining things to me?" This is the exact line Charles needs for bringing up one example after another of Clay's requests for help and input.

But shaming and hurting Clay *isn't* what Charles has in mind; those things are, in his mind, the unavoidable and unfortunate side effects of doing his duty. Charles's concern is with demonstrating to his employees that they can trust him and follow his orders because he is their competent and capable leader, so that the new sales plan he considers necessary for the business will be implemented. He appears to know no other way to accomplish this except by demonstrating that he's able to demolish Clay—violence as first resort. We get no indication that he's even aware of the existence of the obvious alternatives, such as demonstrating to the others how a challenge like Clay's could be skillfully turned aside and made harmless. If Clay understands all this, he will be able to consider the attacks with rational detachment, ignore the bait, and respond appropriately. Like this:

Charles: "If you REALLY wanted to get ahead in this world, you wouldn't make me spend half my time exPLAINing things to you!"

Clay: "I do want to get ahead, Charlie; it matters a lot to me. And that's why I want to be sure I haven't misunderstood what you're proposing."

or

"Getting ahead is very important to me, Charlie. And that's why I want to be sure I haven't misunderstood what's being proposed."

Neither of these responses feeds Charles the right line for a verbal battle; neither one sets Clay up for the kind of humiliation he endured in the original scenario. Both responses are appropriate to the situation and nonhostile; neither one implies that Clay approves of the deception.

Given the nature of the question, it's inevitable that these two men will still disagree. If they can avoid a *fight*, however, they will be able to discuss the deceptive language rationally and more neutrally. If the response to Clay's "I want to be sure I haven't misunderstood" indicates to him that he *hasn't* misunderstood—which means that discussing it further in the meeting is likely to lead to conflict—Clay can say that he realizes it's not a good time for the discussion and that he'll set up an appointment to do it later. In private, he can then make as strong a case for honesty as possible; he may be able to convince his boss to make the change. Going through with the fight makes that impossible.

It may happen (certainly it happens to me!) that you'll suddenly realize that you've carelessly taken the bait in some VAP and are in the middle of a VAPping match. When that happens, please remember that you always have the option of refusing to follow the action chain to its dreary end. No rule of English is violated if you just say this:

"Wait—this is all wrong! Let's stop and start over. Tell me again what you wanted to talk to me about."

This may be enough to get your attacker to give up or shift to Leveling. If not, if what you get next is a new VAP, you have a second chance to handle it correctly. Ignore the bait, no matter how tempting. Respond to something else, something sheltered in a presupposition, instead. That's all that's required.

WORKOUT SECTION

1. There's a famous story in the New Testament in which Jesus is talking to other guests at the home of Mary and Martha, and Mary is sitting listening to Him instead of helping Martha see to everyone's comfort. Martha behaves childishly, going to Jesus and asking Him to make Martha help her instead. Jesus turns her down, saying that Mary has made the better choice. That is, Martha should do the same thing: sit and listen to Him talk, as Mary is doing. (If the guests complained, she could always have said, "The chance to listen to Jesus comes along very rarely, and I don't intend to miss it." They were adult males; they would have managed.)

Assume that instead of going to Jesus and demanding that He order Mary to change her ways, Martha had behaved in a more grown-up manner. Assume that she called Mary to the kitchen and talked this matter over with her directly. What would the two women have said to each other? Write the dialogue.

2. It's easy to use presuppositions thoughtlessly, out of habit or simple carelessness. For example, a teacher wanting to reassure second graders might say, "Don't worry! Even the FIRST graders can pass THIS test!" That presupposes that there's something wrong with both the first graders and the test, plus indicating to the second graders that they'll be even *more* humiliated if they fail it; it's not a good move. It's also easy to use presuppositions with the deliberate intention to slip the content they shelter past the listener more easily, a strategy that (like all strategies) can be used for both good and bad purposes. For example, I recently read an article in a law enforcement journal saying that a certain percentage of all women admit that their husbands have struck them. The word "admit" presupposes guilt on the part of the one doing the admitting, adding an additional message to this seemingly neutral statistical statement.

The rule for this process is: Anything you don't want to have to argue about should be sheltered in a presupposition. That's why corporations will say "Our new, improved soap is now in the stores!" That sentence presupposes "Our soap is new and improved"; its only claim is that the soap is in the stores, something no one is likely to want to argue about.

Put a page in your Conflict Journal for examples of the use and misuse of presuppositions and begin collecting them for your database.

THOUGHT BITES

1. "In modern times, that lacerating use of language came into the discourse with Vietnam. . . . The Left used the tone first, then the Right picked it up; now it comes easily to almost everybody. The tone is sometimes apocalyptic and always judgmental, and its essential component is the sneer" (Hamill, "End Game," 1994, 92).

Do you agree? Did the current uncivil discourse begin with the Vietnam War?

2. "Violence in any form—physical, sexual, psychological, or verbal—is sinful" (The Council of Roman Catholic Bishops, quoted in Briggs, "U.S. Bishops," 1992).

3. "Peace is a habit of *mind,* a way of seeing, the will to make harmony succeed. We have made mistrust and coercion our habit of mind, and built our civilization on the balance of power" (Easwaran, "Three Harmonies," 1991, 50).

4. "Within Christianity—a faith based on the life and teachings of the 'Prince of Peace'—a detailed theology defining and severely limiting the justification of war has existed since the fifth century. . . . But over the centuries, Christians have sharply disagreed on how to put the theory into practice. Today, there is little consensus among religious leaders on how the Persian Gulf conflict—or any modern war—can be justified" (Sheler, "Holy War Doctrine," 1991, 55).

5. "The truth is that we need a lot of lies to get from one day to the next. If we began telling each other the truth, what do you think would happen to the American way of life?" (Warren G. Howells, quoted in Lapham, "Notebook," 1995, 8).

Try answering banker Howells's question: What would happen to "the American way of life" if we insisted on telling the truth? Is lying the only possible way to preserve it or is there some better choice?

CHAPTER NINE

DRAWING LINES OF VERBAL CONDUCT

A wholesome tongue is a tree of life.
Proverbs 15:4

In some of the previous chapters we've looked at verbal conflicts about extremely serious matters such as stealing and teenage drinking. In such contexts, everyone recognizes the distress felt by the people involved in the conflict, and everyone considers that distress valid. In other cases, however, the first reaction is often an "Oh, it's only. . . ." response. We're now going to consider one of those "it's only" cases: "Oh, it's only gossip!"

Whether a specific and unambiguous "Thou shalt not gossip" commandment exists depends on how you *define* gossip. One person's "malicious lie" is another person's "harmless speculation." Is gossip a trivial pastime that no rational adult should be concerned about, just idle talk to keep the social wheels turning, or is it a significant part of verbal violence? By no means is there general agreement about this question. Let's begin our consideration of it with the scenario.

SCENARIO NINE

Phyllis Johnson was so busy, between taking care of her family and volunteering at the hospital, she could rarely find time for socializing. Because she was much more likely to grab a sandwich and work right through the noon hour, lunching at a restaurant in pleasant company was always a treat. But today was apparently *not* going to be pleasant. She had hardly finished the first bite of her salad before Sally Archer started ruining everything.

"You know I go out of my way to be fair," Sally said, "but Brenda is just too **much**! You know what I **mean**?"

"Brenda? Brenda who?" asked one of the other women.

"Brenda Marks. **You** know—**Lew's** wife! Did you hear what she's done **now**?"

Phyllis stared straight ahead, taking one dogged bite after another in silence, while Sally told the sorry tale. In her embroidered version, Brenda's son Tommy had come to school drunk; when the school tried to step in and help, Brenda not only hadn't been grateful, she'd thrown a screaming public fit and threatened a lawsuit; Lew would undoubtedly *beat* Tommy within an inch of his life—everybody knew he abused the boy—and of course everybody also knew that if Brenda had any backbone at all she would have walked out on Lew ten years ago. Sally's own marriage had lasted only a few months, but that didn't hold her back; she never hesitated to give marital advice to others.

Phyllis waited tensely for someone else at the table to object. It didn't happen. Some of her friends were even joining in with "Really?" and "Good grief!" and questions that egged Sally on. *This is all wrong,* Phyllis thought, dismayed. *Sally's knocking herself out to turn the story into a soap opera, and she's exaggerating like mad! But what should I say?*

Sally helped her out, in the end. "Phyllis," she said, "I'll bet you know **lots** of the gory details—your husband's one of the people Brenda's taking to court! How about sharing with the **rest** of us?"

Phyllis hesitated, but when one of the others said, "Come on, Phyllis. What did Brenda actually **say** to Hal?" she put down her fork and spoke up.

"I don't think we ought to talk about Brenda behind her back," she said tensely. "Please—let's change the subject."

In the heavy silence that followed, Phyllis waited, hoping someone else would join in and back her up. But it was Sally who answered. Eyebrows raised, staring at the ceiling, she drawled, "**Now** I remember why I never wanted to go to a slumber party if **Phyllis** was invited!"

"Sally," Phyllis shot back at her through the others' laughter, "you have no reason to talk about me like that just because I think gossip is wicked and wrong! It IS wicked and wrong!"

The sarcastic smile on Sally's face only got wider. She stabbed a piece of grilled chicken with her fork, waved it like a speared victim, and announced, "**Listen**, Goody Two-shoes, gossip is the spice of life! It's the air we breathe! It's the icing on our cake! It's—"

Phyllis couldn't handle it any longer. All she could think of was how much Sally deserved to have *her* entire life—about which Phyllis knew every last tawdry, tacky detail—hauled out and waved around in front of everybody like that piece of grilled chicken. *Forget all that stuff about turning the other cheek!* she thought. *If I don't leave this instant, a complete airing of her life story is exactly what she's going to get from me!*

"Excuse me!" Phyllis said, standing up and grabbing her purse. "I thought this was supposed to be a **friendly** lunch, but I was obviously **wrong**!" She laid enough money beside her untouched plate to cover her check, turned, and marched straight out of the restaurant without looking back.

Behind her she could hear two or three of her friends saying, "Oh, Phyllis, come **on**!" and "Phyllis, you're making a mountain out of a **mole**hill!" And she heard Sally, in an injured tone, protesting that she'd only been making a **joke**, for heaven's sake! She knew she wasn't the only one who could hear them; everybody in the restaurant would be aware that she'd walked out in a huff. Now they'd all be gossiping about *her*!

*I swear I'm going to become a **hermit**!* Phyllis thought as she hurried to her car. *I just don't **understand** people any more!*

It wasn't until evening that she finally asked herself: *Was I making a mountain out of a molehill?* She didn't think so, but she had an uneasy feeling that she might be wrong. After all, everybody else knew as well as she did that Sally Archer wasn't a trustworthy source of information. Maybe it would have been better to ignore the whole thing.

WHAT'S GOING ON HERE?

This is a kind of communication tangle that we all find ourselves involved in once in a while. Different people in this modern world have different ideas about what is and what isn't acceptable language behavior and where lines of conduct should be drawn. Even in a group of people who know one another well and consider themselves good friends, differences of opinion over seemingly minor matters can be large enough to cause significant trouble—including embarrassing public altercations like the one in the scenario.

POINTS OF VIEW

Some of Phyllis's concern is because she knows that Sally made Brenda's problems sound even worse than they are, which is unkind and unfair. But even if Sally had only stated the plain bare facts, Phyllis would have objected. In her opinion, talking negatively about people who aren't present to defend themselves is *wrong*—case closed. But she's a quiet person who intensely dislikes conflict and hates being in the spotlight.

When Sally started bad-mouthing Brenda to their circle of friends, it put Phyllis in a difficult position. She felt obligated to defend the victim of the gossip and make it clear that *she* thought gossip was unacceptable. At the same time, she dreaded the idea of making herself conspicuous and perhaps starting an argument. And she was ashamed of herself for worrying about that possibility instead of doing what she knew was right. Now she feels like a real coward for running away instead of standing her ground and *settling* the matter then and there, and she deeply resents both the fact that Sally put her in such a bind and that none of her other friends came to her aid.

Sally and the others see things differently. They're not vicious people, and they wouldn't deliberately hurt Brenda Marks or anyone else. But when they're alone together, just the circle of friends, they feel that there's nothing wrong with filling one another in on all the town news. They have no plans to spread the resulting stories beyond their group; they just enjoy knowing what's going on and talking it over together, especially when it's as exciting as the tale of the Marks' difficulties. They perceive Phyllis as uptight and prudish, as someone who spoils other people's harmless fun. They agree with Sally that gossip like theirs is "good clean fun," and they resent being made uncomfortable about it just because Phyllis is so prissy.

We're not likely to be able to settle the question of whether gossip is a serious offense or a trivial pastime. My personal opinion, for the record, is that it's wrong. Furthermore, I'm convinced that right *or* wrong, it should be avoided, simply because of the misunderstandings and disagreements it so often leads to. But our concern is with the two problems Phyllis faced:

1. How to stand up for her beliefs without creating a scene and spoiling the occasion for everyone present.
2. How to turn the other cheek in response to Sally's slap without appearing to approve of the gossip about Brenda.

Her solution—delivering one sarcastic smart crack and then fleeing the scene without looking back—was obviously a bad choice.

A number of things went wrong here; we'll go through some of those problems later in this chapter. But first, let's focus our attention on a single aspect of the scenario that we all need to be far more familiar with than we ordinarily are. I want to focus on the powerful language device known as *metaphor*. As in "Gossip is the spice of life," and "Gossip is the icing on our cake."

A COMMUNICATION TECHNIQUE: USING THE POWER OF METAPHOR

It may be that your previous experience with the word *metaphor* has been in school courses in which you were asked to define it on a test or discuss its use in literary language. If so, you will have learned about it as just one "figure of speech" among other figures of speech—for example, the *simile,* as in "His eyes are like doves." For linguists, metaphor is a more general term. It refers to the entire linguistic process in which we talk about one thing in terms of something else. It uses characteristics the two things share as the linking mechanism.

Far from being "only a figure of speech," the various forms of metaphor have tremendous power in our daily lives—so much power that we need to take time here to explore it at length. Let me set the scene for our discussion this way:

Suppose that a serious summer storm hits your town and causes major damage. You find yourself with no electric lights, no air conditioning, no television or radio, no running water, perhaps with no way to get to a store and no way to cook or refrigerate food. When that happens, it's customary to say "This is a disaster, and I am a victim"—a pair of metaphors—and to demand help urgently. *However, people will pay good money, and make plans months in advance, to do something that is called "going camping."*

Think about that for a minute, please. "Going camping" usually involves the same conditions as those imposed by a severe storm: no lights, no TV, no way to cook conveniently, no store nearby, no running water, and so on. But we don't say "This is a disaster, and I am a victim," and we don't demand rescue. We *enjoy* going camping. Clearly, our distress is independent of that set of conditions. In this sense, we most assuredly do create our own reality.

One member of my family grew up in Laos and had the misfortune to spend more than a year in a refugee camp. He finds the idea of voluntarily "going camping" almost insane. He does not perceive it as "This is an adventure," or "This is a vacation," but as "This is a disaster."

For many of our actions we can make a decision easily because we're following a specific accepted rule. When we come to a red light while driving a car, we don't have to stop and consider all the pros and cons while we decide whether to stop or not. For many other things we say and do, however, as we've seen in the scenarios in this book, matters are not so clear-cut. Even when there is a biblical commandment for our reference, it's often nothing like "Stop for every red light"; we have to consider, case by case, what the commandment *means*, whether it applies to us, and so on.

We have to make many such troublesome decisions every day of our lives. Rarely do we have time to sit down, list all the relevant factors that enter into them, and carefully consider each alternative. Like it or not, we usually have to decide what we're going to do, fast. *We solve this dilemma most of the time by choosing a metaphor and following its rules, often without any conscious awareness that that's what we're doing.*

Most adult American males use the metaphor of The Football Game for a vast percentage of their decisions about what to do and say. Most adult American women, on the other hand, rely on the metaphor of The Schoolroom. This difference lies behind a multitude of communication problems between the genders, including many gravely serious ones. On a football field it's not a lie to pretend you have the ball when you really don't, or to pretend that you're going to throw the ball to one person and throw it to another instead. In a schoolroom, anything that is false is a lie—period. On the football field, knocking down a member of the other team isn't violence; in a schoolroom, any use of physical force between students is violence—period. Much of the time, when it seems to a woman that a man has no morals and it seems to the man that the woman has no common sense, it's because she's filtering her perceptions through the Schoolroom metaphor and he's filtering his through the Football one. They both agree that lying and violence are wrong, but those words are defined differently in the very different metaphors they're using.

How we feel, and what we do and say, about being fat depends on whether we define fat simply as one possible human body shape (my personal preference) or choose a metaphor as the definition. And *which* metaphor we choose   "Fat is a disability,"

or "Fat is a sin," or "Fat is an illness," or "Fat is a genetic characteristic,"—is crucially important. When we're sick, or interacting with someone who's sick, our behavior revolves around
the metaphor we choose for the illness. "That disease is a punishment for sin" leads to different decisions than "That disease
is a disaster, and people are its helpless victims."

I pointed out to you in the introduction that much of our trouble with the commandment to turn the other cheek and return
good for evil is tightly linked to the power of metaphor for two
reasons:

1. The choice of "I am a warrior" as the metaphor for our
   behavior.
2. The fact that our understanding of the rules and roles and
   scripts in the Warrior metaphor appears to us to be in direct
   conflict with the commandment to turn the other cheek.

This is the source of Phyllis's difficulties in Scenario Nine. As
a Christian, she knows she is not supposed to start fights, and
she knows she is supposed to turn the other cheek when attacked.
On the other hand, she feels that she is obligated—as a warrior
is obligated—to come to the defense of the victim of the gossip, to see justice done on behalf of that victim, and to defend her
own conviction that gossip is immoral. Because she mistakenly
believes that the Warrior metaphor is her only choice and that
the only truly warrior-like response is to slap Sally *back*, she han-
dles her dilemma very badly and ends by feeling that the role she
took in the metaphor this time was not just Loser but Coward.

We make decisions in this fashion constantly. The problem for
our communication with others is that the process, like the rest
of our internal grammar, is usually below the level of our conscious awareness. If asked why we did or said something, we're

likely to say it was because "I felt like it was the only choice I had," or "I didn't know what else to do," or "That's what everybody else does" or something equally vague. We never say anything like "I did it that way because I was perceiving the world through the Warrior metaphor and I was following its rules." Unless people have had their attention explicitly drawn to the way we use metaphors, they—like Phyllis—will be unaware of their real basis for decisions of this kind. Understanding the role metaphors play in our lives (as a result of reading this book, for example) is a major step forward.

It's extremely important, if we are to learn to reason together, to become *aware* that we use metaphors as perceptual filters for making decisions, even when for one reason or another we don't know precisely which metaphor is involved. We will communicate in a quite different way if we are thinking, *He's saying that because he's a liar* than if we're thinking, *He must be operating out of the Football metaphor.* Our attitude toward someone will be very different if we're thinking, *She's attacking me because she hates people like me* than if we're thinking, *She must be operating out of the Warrior metaphor.* Even when we can do no more than remember to ask ourselves, "I wonder what metaphor they're using?" instead of "I wonder what's **wrong** with **them?**", it's progress. Our attitude toward what's being said won't change. We'll dislike it as much as ever. But our attitude toward the *speaker* will be dramatically different, and the chances for more successful communication and less conflict will be greatly increased.

One more thing: Nowhere in the Bible does it say, "Thou shalt choose the Warrior metaphor." Many metaphors appear in the Bible, and the Warrior gets no special treatment. Nowhere in the laws of these United States does it say that we must choose one metaphor rather than another. This is a case in which we are free—to make poor choices or to make good ones. I'm not free to say "Bats are birds," because "A bat is a mammal" is not a metaphor but a statement of fact. Our lack of awareness about the way we use metaphors has caused us to behave as though metaphors were statements of fact, too. They're not. We *choose* them.

I have no illusions about being able to persuade people to abandon the Warrior metaphor. Despite the confusion it brings to our lives, it controls so much of what we do today and is so tightly woven into our culture that making that change is probably impossible. One reason men adopt the Football metaphor is that it's so much *like* the Warrior metaphor. One major reason for women's difficulties today is the vast gulf between the world of the Schoolroom and the world of the Warrior. I do believe, however, that I can persuade people at least to begin *thinking* about all this, and to keep it consciously in mind in their interactions with others. I believe I can persuade them to take another look at what "warrior" means and to remember that war must include the concept of violence as a last—not first or second or tenth—resort, used reluctantly. And I strongly suggest that when we humans disagree over issues that are not a matter of life or death (gossip, for example) we choose a metaphor that doesn't automatically call up the rules of combat in our memories.

I suggest that in all such situations we choose the Carpenter rather than the Warrior. Jesus was at one time a carpenter; it's a skilled and respected role. Instead of choosing sides and insisting that when we disagree one of us must come out the Winner and the other the Loser, we can do what carpenters do: We can work together. When we are trying to build a foundation for agreement, as carpenters build foundations for houses, winning and losing are irrelevant. Even if we only manage to agree to *dis*-agree, we would be working together instead of fighting. That would *guarantee* fewer slaps on fewer cheeks and help us be better stewards of our limited stores of moral strength and courage.

ANOTHER LOOK
AT SCENARIO NINE

Remember that it's far better to *prevent* conflict than to repair it. Suppose that when Phyllis found herself in the situation described in the scenario, instead of approaching it as a Warrior she chose the Carpenter metaphor. In that case her goal would not be to win. Winning has nothing at all to do with building, whether what you're building is a consensus or a barn. Her question would not have been "How can I win this argument?" but "How can I build good feeling within this group? What can I do to keep this situation from collapsing around us?" With that point of view, she could have used the techniques you've learned in this book as a way of putting an end to the gossip *before* it became the subject of a struggle. For example:

Sally: "Well, the **first** thing that happened is that Brenda's kid—Tommy—came to school **drunk.** Can you believe it? **Drunk!**"

Phyllis: "The problem of teenage drinking is getting worse all the time. In fact, I read somewhere that almost a third of all teenagers drink, and most of them are binge drinkers."

Janice: "Really? What does that mean, exactly? It doesn't mean the kids go on actual binges, the way real alcoholics do, surely?"

Phyllis: "No, I think it means that instead of just having a drink or two, those teenagers deliberately keep drinking until they're drunk. Getting drunk is the **goal.**"

Sally: "But that's awful!"

Phyllis: "Isn't it? Just imagine—"

What Phyllis does in this revision is simply to head the conversation in a slightly different direction. Notice, however, that she didn't change the subject; she didn't violate any of the rules of conversation or cause Sally to lose face. She wasn't trying to *win*. She took the topic Sally had introduced, which was a specific example of teenage drinking, and shifted it, with a Computer Mode sentence, to the *abstract* problem of teenage drinking. This is like a carpenter who notices that a board someone else nailed up is going to fall, and who—instead of taking an ax and chopping the board to bits or using the ax to hit the other carpenter—expertly adds another nail in a different spot. With any luck at all, that board will stay where it belongs; with any luck at all, Phyllis's group of friends will switch to a discussion of teenage drinking or teenagers in general, and Sally's gossip will never enter the conversation.

But what if Sally persists? What if she waits for the first gap in the discussion, takes back the floor, and says, "Now, as I was saying . . ." followed by a description of the public temper fit that Brenda Marks is alleged to have thrown and the threat of a lawsuit? Then Phyllis repeats the same maneuver again:

Phyllis: "You know, people in the U.S. are so lawsuit-happy that it's becoming a serious problem."

This utterance once again acknowledges Sally's topic and *builds* on it, while at the same time shifting away from the gossip about Brenda Marks and her family. In the unlikely event that Sally should actually challenge her on her strategy—"Phyllis, **why** do you keep trying to stop me from talking about Brenda Marks and what she's gotten herself into now?"—that would be a perfect opportunity for Phyllis to speak up for her beliefs. She could then say, "Since you asked me, Sally, it's because Brenda's not here to defend herself and her family. That's not fair." Chances are excellent that in that situation one or more of the other women would speak up and agree with her. It's more likely, however, that in each case the conversation will simply shift from Sally's attempts to dish the dirt to the more abstract topics Phyllis has introduced.

When we see eighteen-month-old Billy preparing to whack sixteen-month-old Jackie over the head with a plastic truck, we don't take the truck and hit *Billy* with it. We take the truck away from him, gently, so that he can't proceed with the attack, and we distract him from that purpose by suggesting some other activity. That same strategy is entirely appropriate for dealing with adults who are determined to use language as a weapon. Pick up the topic the abusive adult intended to use to do damage, so that the attack stops, and introduce a distraction.

Suppose, however, that Phyllis doesn't use this strategy and that she finds herself on the verge of verbal combat. Then what alternative does she have? Assume that the scenario follows its original course right up to this point:

Sally: "**Now** I remember why I never wanted to go to a slumber party if **Phyllis** was invited!"

In the original, Phyllis responded to this hostile smart crack from Sally by hitting back. That's not indicated except as a last resort, and she has other choices she hasn't yet tried. For example:

Phyllis: "You're absolutely right, Sally. I was never any fun to be around when I felt that what was going on was wrong, and I haven't changed." [Leveling]

or

Phyllis: "Many people have a hard time enjoying themselves

179

when they feel that what's going on around them is wrong. That's one of the common challenges in human communication." [Computing]

Neither of these responses feeds the hostility loop that Sally was trying to set up. In the Leveling response, Phyllis finds a portion of Sally's challenge that she can agree with, and does so, while handing back the conversational turn. In the Computing response, she lowers the level of hostility by moving from the personal quarrel to an abstract issue, without changing the subject or using hostile language. Both responses belong to the Carpenter metaphor: Their goal is not to win but to build a foundation for agreement. Phyllis's choice between the two will depend on her personal judgment about the situation, the people involved, and other real-world factors. What matters is that these two choices (and many more that I could construct) are available for her to try before she has to even *begin* thinking about hitting back at Sally.

There's nothing exotic or difficult about the changes I just made. Every one of you reading this book would be as likely to think of these or similar revisions as I am—*if, and only if, you had stepped out of the Warrior metaphor and into the Carpenter metaphor.* That single change is all that's required.

WORKOUT SECTION

1. Metaphor is the very heart of the act of worship, because the human mind cannot imagine God. The only way we can get close to the Divine day by day is by imagining divine metaphors and using them for our "godtalk"—God as Father; God as a mighty fortress; Jesus as Prince of Peace; Mother Teresa describing herself as a "pencil in God's hand." It may seem to you that such metaphors have no place in your Conflict Journal; I suggest

that they belong there, and that you set up a special page for collecting and analyzing them. Some of the most potentially hostile language interactions that we are ever likely to become involved in are those in which we are obliged to try to explain or defend our religious beliefs. For that sort of interaction, you *need* good metaphors, together with a deep and complete understanding of what they mean to you.

2. Work on metaphor is never wasted and will pay you back for your effort many times over. Set up pages in your Conflict Journal for working with the metaphors in your own life.

    a. Set up a "Personal Metaphor Log" in which you write down metaphors you hear yourself say, to others or in self-talk. Do you say things like "This place is a disaster area," or "This job is a killer," or "My boss is a pain in the neck," or "It's a jungle out there," or "She makes my blood boil"? (Often your metaphors won't appear in the exact "X is Y" form; "This job is killing me" is just another way to say, "This job is a killer.") A constant flood of negative metaphors contaminates your language environment and is *bad* for you. Your mind and body have a strong tendency to take such language literally, and you'd be wise to find positive metaphors to replace the negative ones. Do you perceive yourself as a disaster victim or are you someone who's going camping?

    To search for more positive metaphors, you follow two simple steps. Your metaphor will be "X is Y," (sometimes "X is like Y"). Write down the set of features that are the *reason* you call a particular X a Y— the reason that you say "This job is a killer," or "This room is a swamp." Then ask yourself, "What else has

181

those same features and is not so negative?"

b. Set up a log for *non*religious metaphors that you hear or read, so that when you suddenly find yourself needing one for an upcoming language interaction you have a collection to choose from or get ideas from. If you don't write them down as you come across them, you'll forget them.

c. Set up a Metaphor Incidents Log in which you record incidents in which metaphors were a major factor. Keep track of incidents in your life in which someone else's use of a metaphor had powerful effects, negative or positive, on what happened; keep track of incidents in which a metaphor of your own did the same. For example: For many years I had a strongly negative reaction to people who invited me to their home and then left a television set turned on low while we were talking. I understood that to mean that they weren't really interested in our conversation, and that belief was reflected in my behavior toward my hosts. Then one day I read Camille Paglia's claim that the television set is the flickering fire on the hearth in today's homes. My attitude changed *instantly*! Suddenly I—a member of the *radio* generation—understood what was going on. I wouldn't have expected people to put out a fire in their fireplace while we were talking; why should I expect them to turn off their TV set? The television set in the background still bothered me as much as it ever had, but I no longer perceived it as an insult. *My feelings and behavior toward my hosts changed dramatically for the better.* No amount of logical argument or emotional pleading can change attitudes that fast and that permanently; only metaphors have that power. Nothing is more useful in a disagreement than a metaphor that lets you make your meaning clear like that, instantly and completely.

3. Sometimes metaphors fail to bring about the *shazam!* effect described above because they include some element that the speaker hasn't thought through carefully or doesn't realize is there. For example, in *The Father Book* [Minirth et al. 1992] the authors discuss *a grandfather* on page 254 as "a mantle, a shawl, a wraparound" that lets a grandchild feel "nested inside" the family. The image is beautiful, but it's flawed. If you list the features that identify mantles and shawls and wraparounds, the problem will leap out at you. Who wears a mantle? Who wears a shawl or wraparound? In either case, is the individual that comes immediately to mind a grandfather? (This is one constant problem with the efforts to use more "inclusive" language. You can't just convert "The Lord is my shepherd" to "The Lady is my shepherdess," however inclusive it might be, because what the word "shepherdess" brings immediately to mind is something along the lines of Little Bo-Peep.)

4. Writing of Jesus, William Johnson Everett (Everett, *Christian Century,* 1989, 504) described Him as one "whose presidency was powered by listening, whose republic was founded in covenant bonding, and whose election was rooted in self-sacrifice." Does this "Jesus is a President" metaphor work for you? Why or why not?

THOUGHT BITES

1. "It is entirely possible that angels are best understood as a metaphor to describe God's presence among us" [Wael, "Unlearning Skepticism," 1988, 827].

2. "Repeated recourse to the language of war makes it harder to love our enemies—and it is already hard to do so—because it inflames angry feelings. . . . It leaves no room for nuanced positions, or for middle ground" (Woodbridge, "Casualties," 1995, 22).

3. *With regard to choosing metaphors for such things as illnesses, overweight or short stature, character traits, and the like:*

"Some genetic researchers do posit genetic causality not only for . . . illnesses such as manic depression and schizophrenia but for morally disapproved behavior such as stealing. If the latter sort of behavior is ultimately caused by specific genes, then both free will and moral responsibility are canceled" (Nelson, "Genetics," 1988, 389).

When this was written, the idea of such "genetic causality" was still abstract and remote. Today, with the progress of the Human Genome Project, it suddenly is terrifyingly real and near. The phrase "only a figure of speech" is obviously an error.

CHAPTER TEN

REASONING TOGETHER: LANGUAGE AND MORAL UNDERSTANDING

Death and life are in the power of the tongue.
Proverbs 18:21

Our lives would be simpler and easier if every moral decision were a clear-cut yes or no like the law for stopping at red lights. Situations in which you have to ask yourself whether to stop at a red light or go straight through it are so rare as to be almost nonexistent. But many, perhaps most, moral decisions are far more ambiguous. This problem isn't limited to relativists (those who believe that no absolute moral standards exist) or to those whose policy is "If it feels good, do it." Even the strictest literalist, firmly convinced that there is one set of absolute laws that has no exceptions, will have to struggle with *linguistic* problems. Words aren't like numbers; words in combination—unlike two times eleven—multiply the possible meanings. Two and eleven will always be exactly the same no matter where you encounter them, but language has an inescapable "fuzziness" that is independent of both faith and doctrine.

Take lying, for instance. The Bible commands us not to lie, not just once but in many different verses. Does that mean that going along with the customs of Santa Claus or the Easter Bunny is sinful? Does it mean that when your neighbor proudly shows you the new baby and asks, "Isn't she beautiful?" you're morally obligated to answer with a truthful, "No, based on my previous experience with newborns, your baby is actually rather ugly"? Does it mean that the life of a spy or an undercover police officer is, by definition, a life of sin? No? Why not? By what logic does "If I don't lie, I can't catch drug dealers" cancel the commandment? What about the lawyer who, though believing a defendant is guilty, must defend that client in court? We have a clear "just war" doctrine, hammered out with painstaking effort over centuries; we have no corresponding doctrine of "the just lie." *It's not easy.*

Whenever good people, and devout people come down strongly on opposite sides of serious moral questions, misunderstandings are inevitable unless great care is taken with language. We need to consider ways in which that challenge of taking great care can be met. In this chapter, therefore, we're going to examine the difficulty of communicating about one issue that leads to bitter controversy in our society today: *divorce*.

The Bible says quite clearly that we may not divorce a spouse except for sexual infidelity; equally clearly, many Christians today either ignore that rule or believe that it no longer holds. More than half of all marriages in the U.S. now end in divorce. There's no way that such a situation can exist without the potential for conflict between believers on opposite sides of the issue.

In Scenario Ten, Phyllis Johnson knows that her close friend, Elizabeth Hayward, has decided to get a divorce because her abusive husband makes life a constant misery for her and for their three young sons. Phyllis knows Elizabeth has agonized over her decision and is heartsick over it; the two women have spent many hours struggling with the issue. Counseling, both through a pastoral counselor and a professional therapist, has already been tried, with no success; if anything, it seemed to make matters worse. Nevertheless—because Phyllis believes that divorce other than for infidelity is forbidden to Christians—she feels that she *must* try again to convince her friend to change her mind and stay in her marriage. We're going to look at two versions of this scenario, and then we'll discuss them both.

SCENARIO TEN, VERSION A

"Elizabeth," Phyllis said, with all the conviction and passion she could muster, "I'm so sorry. . . . I know how unhappy you are. But I don't have a choice—I **have** to try to get you to change your mind! I **can't** just stand by and watch you ruin your own life, and your children's lives, without doing **every** last thing I **can** to **stop** you! Please . . . let's talk it over, just one more time. If you—"

"Stop it!" Elizabeth said sharply. "Just STOP it!" Tears were streaming down her face. "How can you be so cruel? Please, Phyllis, you KNOW how hard this is for me—PLEASE don't talk about it any more!"

"I can't do that," Phyllis said sadly. "I can't simply let it go! We have to **talk** about it, Elizabeth! We have to sit down and—"

Elizabeth interrupted her again, fiercely, "And you call yourself my **friend**! How can you DO this to me? You KNOW this is tearing me apart! You KNOW that! Don't you have any human feelings at ALL?"

Phyllis reached out to gather the other woman into her arms, but Elizabeth backed away, her face distorted with her pain and anger.

"NO!" she shouted. "Don't you TOUCH me! I hate you, Phyllis! You don't know ANYthing about what I'm going through! YOU with your wonderful, kind, responsible husband and your loving marriage and your perfect life! It's EASY for YOU to stand there and judge me! You are a NARROW-minded, HEARTless WOman, and I want you out of my house—NOW!"

"Elizabeth, PLEASE!" Phyllis pleaded. "You're my dearest friend! I wouldn't hurt you for the world, but I **cannot** stand aside and watch you—"

Elizabeth marched to the door and flung it open wide. "Get out!" she spat. "GET OUT! Get OUT of my HOUSE!"

Now Phyllis was crying, too. *How could this be happening?* Sick at heart, with no idea what else she could do, she threw up her hands and hurried past Elizabeth, out the door, and down the front walk. Behind her, the door slammed, *hard,* like a gunshot in the quiet evening air.

What have I done? Phyllis asked herself miserably. *And what can I do now to* fix *it?*

This scenario shows us no useful communication at all, just an emotional scene between two people in great distress. Suppose that at least one of them had made a greater effort to control her emotions and maintain some degree of calm. Would the encounter have ended differently? Let's look at another version of the scenario and find out. Phyllis has challenged her friend about the decision to divorce; Elizabeth has pleaded with her to drop the subject; and Phyllis has said no—she can't let it pass, they *must* discuss it again.

SCENARIO TEN, VERSION B

Elizabeth sighed and wiped away her tears. "All right," she said. She sat down on her couch and waved at a chair facing her.

"I've heard it all before, but I'll let you say it one more time if you must."

And she did listen. She sat silently while Phyllis explained, as she had explained before, over and over again, that the divorce was forbidden, that it was a sin, that she *must* not do it, no matter how good her reasons seemed to her to be.

When Phyllis finally stopped, Elizabeth asked, "Is that the end?"

"Yes!" Phyllis answered. "Yes . . . I don't know any other way to say it or any other words to use."

"All right. I've listened to you. I haven't interrupted you even once. Now I want **you** to listen to **me**, without interrupting."

"Of **course**," Phyllis said. "Of course I will!"

Elizabeth clasped her hands in her lap, leaned toward her friend, and began talking.

"Just imagine, Phyllis," she said, "that you found me living in a filthy place with polluted water and spoiled food, with toxic chemical waste piling up outside in the yard. Suppose that happened. Would you tell me I had to stay there, in spite of the danger to my children's health and the danger to *their* children's health in the future? Or would you tell me that it was my duty as a mother to get my kids **out** of that terrible situation?"

"I don't understand why you're asking me that," Phyllis said slowly. "I don't understand what it has to do with your decision to divorce Larry."

"Let me tell you what it has to do with it!" Elizabeth said. "There is massive evidence that the kind of verbal abuse the boys and I live with every day is just as poisonous as polluted food and water and toxic waste. You can't see it and you can't smell it, but it's every bit as dangerous. And that's not all! It has—"

"But, Elizabeth—" Phyllis began, but her friend raised a cautioning hand.

"You agreed to hear me out without interrupting me," Elizabeth reminded her.

"Sorry," Phyllis said. "Go on."

"It has also been proved that the one thing abusive parents have in common is that when they were children they watched one of **their** parents abuse the other in their home. Toxic talk is like a genetic disease—it gets passed on from generation to generation. Phyllis—I live, with my children, in a toxic waste dump. Isn't it my responsibility as a mother to get my boys out of this terrible situation? Out of danger? Isn't that what I am obligated, as their mother, to do?"

"It's not the same **thing!**"

"No?" Elizabeth asked her. "Explain that, Phyllis! Explain to me why it's not the same. What's the **difference?**" Phyllis sat there staring at her friend for a minute, wondering what on earth to say; the best she could do was a furious, "That's not FAIR! You're deliberately putting me into a TRAP!"

Elizabeth's eyebrows went up. "And what do you call **my** situation, Phyllis? Would you like to change places with me? The trap I'm in, for the one you're in?"

"Elizabeth, you're not yourSELF!" Phyllis heard herself saying then; she felt both foolish and useless. "I'll come back and talk to you later!"

"No, you won't," Elizabeth told her grimly. "You've had your chance—and it's the **last one you get.** Don't you **ever** bring this subject up with me again!"

Phyllis hurried out the door, her heart pounding so loudly that it seemed to her that the other woman must be able to hear it too.

Behind her she could hear Elizabeth laughing the high, thin laughter that goes with far too much emotional strain. *What have*

I done? she asked herself anxiously. *And what can I do now to* fix *it?*

WHAT'S GOING ON HERE?

Both versions of this scenario show us two women in great pain, each trying to do what she feels she **must** do, struggling with language that doesn't seem to be adequate to her communication task.

POINTS OF VIEW

The points of view in this scenario are obvious. Elizabeth believes that for her children's sake she must divorce their father. She considers that her duty as a mother who loves her children and protects them. Making the decision to divorce Larry was agonizing, and following through on it will take every ounce of strength she has. She bitterly resents Phyllis's persistent interference. It seems to her that now that the decision has been made, her friend should either help her or—if moral revulsion makes that impossible—at least get out of the way and let her do what she must do, in peace. Phyllis sees things very differently; her perception is that if she fails to convince Elizabeth to stay in her marriage she has failed in *every* way—as a woman, as a friend, and as a Christian. She feels that she must try again and keep on trying.

What Elizabeth perceives as interference and cruelty, Phyllis perceives as love; what Phyllis perceives as wickedness, Elizabeth perceives as love. How, with such different views of reality, can the two communicate with one another about the issue?

Our first step is to acknowledge that by any standard Phyllis's opening utterance was hostile language. That was unquestionably a serious mistake. Once that mistake was made, however, the scenario was set in motion, and Elizabeth had to decide how to respond.

Our culture teaches us only three ways to respond to hostile language:

1. Counterattacking, by hitting back
2. Pleading
3. Debating

In the two versions of Scenario Ten we see all three of these methods of response in action—and we see that none of them *works*. Phyllis opens the interaction with an utterance so hostile in both its presuppositions and its intonation that it is like striking a blow with an open hand. And Elizabeth uses all three traditional methods to respond.

Counterattacking (Version A):
- "Stop it! Just STOP it! How can you be so CRUEL?"
- "You KNOW this is tearing me apart! You KNOW that! Don't you have any human feelings at ALL?"
- "Don't you TOUCH me! I hate you, Phyllis! You don't know ANYthing about what I'm going through! YOU with your wonderful, kind, responsible husband . . ."
- "You are a NARROW-minded HEARTless WOman."
- "GET OUT! Get OUT of my HOUSE!"

Pleading (Version A):
- "Please, Phyllis, you KNOW how hard this is for me— PLEASE don't talk about it any more!"
- "How can you DO this to me?"

Debating (Version B):
- "All right, I've heard it all before, but I'll let you say it one more time if you must."

- "I've listened to you. Now I want **you** to listen to **me**." [Followed by the logical argument comparing pollution of the physical environment with linguistic pollution.]
- "Explain to me why it's not the same. What's the **difference?**"
- "And what do you call **my** situation, Phyllis? Would you like to change places . . . ?"

Both versions of Scenario Ten demonstrate a nearly total failure of communication. A speaker who hasn't been able to achieve a communication goal can usually at least say, "Well, anyway, I **feel** better now that I've gotten that off my **chest!**" A speaker who has attacked someone verbally just to satisfy a need for attention will usually feel better afterward, no matter how unpleasant that attention turned out to be. But Phyllis doesn't have either of those consolations. She feels *worse,* not better. And in both versions, Elizabeth is equally without consolation.

You will have spotted many problems in the two versions of the scenario, and you are now aware of a set of techniques for tackling those problems. Let's review what we know, and tie it all together now, by carefully analyzing the interaction between Phyllis and Elizabeth and constructing a new, and more useful, version.

STRATEGIC ANALYSIS
AND REVISION

In this section we will focus our attention not on the moral issue itself but on how well the two speakers in the scenario are able to communicate with one another *about* the moral issue. Words in this section such as *right* and *wrong* and *mistake,* therefore, refer to language strategies and techniques, not to morality. The communication problem is clear:

- Some Christians believe that divorce other than for infidelity is forbidden and evil; other Christians, equally devout, disagree.
- If we are ever to resolve the issue, we have to be able to *talk* to one another about it.

Let's run through the set of communication techniques that have been presented in this book to see what role they have played in Scenario Ten.

True Listening

The conflict in this scenario isn't one that could have been solved by better listening. Because the issue of divorce matters so much to both speakers, and because they care so deeply about one another, they are listening *very* closely. So closely, in fact, that no word either says will ever be forgotten by the other.

Using Miller's Law

It's not clear that either speaker is using Miller's Law, however. To do so, Phyllis would have to assume—temporarily, for purposes of discussion—that the sentence "Divorce for verbal and emotional abuse is acceptable" is true, and then she would have to try to imagine what it could be true of. Elizabeth would have to assume, in the same fashion, that the sentence "Divorce for verbal and emotional abuse is wicked" is true, and try to imagine what *it* could be true of. Neither woman in version A seems able to set aside her personal convictions long enough to consider the issue with the detachment that Miller's Law requires. And in version B, although Elizabeth takes a step toward detachment by bringing up her logical arguments, Phyllis is unable or unwilling to follow her lead; instead, she runs away.

It's important to realize that just reasoning together about an issue is *not* equivalent to abandoning your beliefs for the beliefs of others or letting them "win." If you are right, giving other opinions a fair hearing poses no threat to your beliefs. The better you understand why you hold your beliefs, the better able you are to explain and defend them, the stronger they become, and the more likely it is that you may be able to persuade others to share them. If you're wrong, on the other hand, you need to *know* that you are.

For example, I am a pacifist. I truly believe that there is *never* a situation in which it is morally right for one person to kill another. When people find this out, they always ask me whether I can imagine a situation in which I would be willing to kill another person. And I am always able to apply Miller's Law and answer them truthfully: If someone were about to torture another human being in my presence or with my personal knowledge, and if I could find no other way to prevent the torture, I would be willing to kill to stop it.

That answer doesn't mean I am abandoning my beliefs. It doesn't mean I consider the sentence, "Killing another human being is sometimes morally right," to be true—although I have examined the possibility that it might be, for purposes of discussion. It means that I know where the limits of my convictions are and that I am not afraid to talk about those limits. It means that I trust the strength of my convictions enough to be willing to listen respectfully to what others have to say on the subject. So far, despite the arguments I've heard, I would still consider killing the torturer a moral failure on my part, and I would still be deeply ashamed of my inability to find some other solution to the problem. That doesn't mean I can't talk about the issue and discuss it with others.

And it doesn't mean that I "lose" when I admit that a situation exists in which I know I would be unable to act according to my beliefs. *That would be true for me only if I chose the* disagreement is combat *metaphor.* Like every other human being, I am free to reject that metaphor, and I do. Winning and losing have absolutely no relevance here.

Phyllis and Elizabeth would have had a far better chance to accomplish their communication goals if they had both had sufficient respect for the strength of their convictions to use Miller's Law.

SENSORY MODES

The sensory modes weren't a source of problems in Scenario Ten, but they're not irrelevant. We need to notice how they functioned in this case.

Phyllis and Elizabeth obviously share the same sensory mode rankings: They both put touch first, followed by hearing. This may be one reason why they're such close friends; ordinarily they would find it very easy to communicate with one another. If this weren't true, we can be sure that the highly emotional nature of their interaction would tend to lock them into their dominant modes. Whenever that happens, it helps for one speaker to use the technique of sensory mode matching and shift to "speak the same language" as the other speaker. But helpful as sensory mode matching is, this scenario shows that it's not a panacea. The fact that there's no sensory mode conflict in the scenario is not enough to bring about agreement or to prevent the total communication breakdown. The issue is too highly charged for that to be possible.

SATIR MODES

In both versions, Phyllis makes the mistake of opening the interaction with Blaming. She sets up negative expectations and creates tension. She uses the sequence "ruin your own life, and your children's lives" with all its negative connotations. She relies heavily on very personal vocabulary, and she adds emphatic stresses to *four* words in a single sentence, saying, "I **can't** just stand by and watch you ruin your own life and your children's lives, without doing **every** last thing I **can** to **stop** you!"

It could have been worse. She could have made those extra stresses even stronger. She could have used more words from the semantic field of evil and sin. But the opening is bad enough as it stands, and it has the predictable result: Elizabeth responds immediately with equally hostile language, using Blaming and Placating.

THREE-PART MESSAGES

Neither Phyllis nor Elizabeth uses three-part messages. Except for Elizabeth's one careful request—"I've listened to you . . . and now I want you to listen to me, without interrupting"—they give each other direct and open commands.

This is counterproductive. Every expression of a desire for change in someone else's behavior is best made as a three-part message and has far greater chances of succeeding in that form; the more emotional the atmosphere, the truer that is. There were plenty of appropriate places for three-part messages. Phyllis might have said, "When you order me to leave your house, I feel both afraid and sad, because an order like that could end a friendship forever." Elizabeth might have said, "When you say that I am going to ruin my children's lives, I feel heartbroken, because my children mean more to me than anything else in this world." It is *always* a wise move to use a three-part message as a strategy for working toward agreement, especially when emotions are running high, if only because it demonstrates that you have no interest in causing the other person to lose face.

Verbal Attack Patterns

The verbal attack patterns don't occur in either version of the scenario. That may seem surprising, because Phyllis and Elizabeth are so intensely emotional. There are two reasons why they aren't used. First, both speakers are so emotionally upset that they can't manage even the rough-hewn subtlety of the VAPs. They just hack and slash away at each other in open verbal combat. Second, the most common use of VAPs is as a way to get and hold attention, as a kind of linguistic power trip. Because neither Phyllis nor Elizabeth is trying to fill a need for attention, that doesn't happen here; it isn't that sort of interaction. And Phyllis really is trying to hurt her friend as little as possible with her words, which makes the attack patterns unlikely.

The closest thing to an example of a VAP comes from Elizabeth, when she asks, "How can you DO this to me?" But we have every reason to believe that she is adding the extra emphasis to "do" not to carry a message of hostility but because she needs it to express the *intensity* of her feelings.

Metaphors

The metaphors that govern both versions of the scenario—not moral failings or rhetorical inadequacies—are the primary reason for the communication breakdown between Phyllis and Elizabeth. They are *disagreement is combat,* and its companion, *I am a warrior*. The moment they were chosen, failure could only have been avoided by blind chance or divine inspiration, neither of which materialized. The communication choices made were dictated by the metaphor's rules and were the language not of love or friendship but of war.

Phyllis perceived herself as a Warrior who was obligated to prevent her friend from destroying both the lives of her children and her own life; she felt obligated to keep Elizabeth from committing a sin with terrible consequences. Those were her goals. She came nowhere close to accomplishing either of them.

Elizabeth perceived herself as a Warrior who was under fierce attack and was obligated to defend herself and her household. By the rules of the Warrior metaphor, we have to say that she did pretty well, because she was able to drive her attacker from the battlefield. She "won." Never mind how little that has to do with anything that matters in this sad situation. Never mind the fact that it may well mean she has destroyed a friendship she will need desperately in the hard times ahead of her. Nevertheless, under Warrior rules, driving away the marauder—Phyllis—is a partial triumph.

The final result of all this? Elizabeth is like the soldier who has driven away the enemy by burning everything in his own village and its surrounding countryside to the ground. We call this an "empty" or "hollow" victory, but we don't call it "losing."

We can do better than this. Let's turn again to the language in the scenario and see how we could rewrite it, using what we've learned, so that it might end less negatively.

ANOTHER LOOK AT SCENARIO TEN

Here is the utterance Phyllis started with:

Phyllis: "I'm so sorry. . . . I know how unhappy you are. But I don't have a choice—I **have** to try to get you to change your mind! I **can't** just stand by and watch you ruin your own life, and your children's lives, without doing **every** last thing I **can** to **stop** you! Please . . . let's talk it over, just one more time. If you—"

This is about as bad a beginning as could be imagined, short of hitting Elizabeth over the head with a club. Phyllis has a negative message to deliver, and she feels obligated to take that step. "I don't have a choice," she says—the "just war" justification. But she also has a goal, and it's not just to express her feelings. Her goal is to persuade Elizabeth to change her mind. She has no hope of accomplishing that unless and until she can convince her friend to *listen* to her. And she can't do *that* by shaping her message as criticism and moralizing and threatening. Furthermore, complaining that she has no choice is absurd; she could have begun with something else entirely. For example:

Phyllis: "Elizabeth, nothing is more ridiculous than a person who keeps going over the same thing again and again, never getting anywhere, and who just won't give up. But I care enough about you to be more than willing to risk being ridiculous. I'd like to get your permission to talk about the divorce again—if you'll let me."

This utterance begins as Computing and then switches to Leveling; it warns Elizabeth that something hurtful is coming and asks for her permission to continue. Now one of two things will happen. Elizabeth will either give the permission or refuse it, *but she won't feel that she has been attacked and that all further communication is impossible.* Either way, Phyllis can then go ahead with what she has to say. If Elizabeth says yes, Phyllis can begin making her case; if she says no, Phyllis is still in a better position than before and less likely to be thrown out of the house. Here's one possibility:

Eliz.: "No, Phyllis, I'm not going to go through that again! My mind's made up, and I know what I have to do. Let it go—**please.**"
Phyllis: "I wish you could have said yes; I'm sorry you didn't

feel that you could. And now I'm asking you to forgive me for going ahead **without** your permission. And I'm asking you to remember that the only thing that could make me do that is the feeling, deep in my heart, that this is an emergency. Elizabeth, the rules are different in emergencies; people have to do things they wouldn't ordinarily do."

Eliz.: "So you're going to **force** me to listen to you?!"

Phyllis: "I might be able to force you to **hear** me. Maybe I could. But there's no way I can force you to **listen**; I know that."

Eliz.: "Then why are you **trying**?"

Phyllis: "Because you matter to me. And because, as I said, this is an emergency."

Eliz.: [Sighs.] "Oh, all right, Phyllis, go ahead and get it over with! But I warn you—you can't change my mind."

Phyllis: "Maybe not, but at least I will have tried."

And what if Elizabeth doesn't take it this well? What if she tries to start a fight? What if she attacks?

Eliz.: "So you're going to FORCE me to listen to you?! And you call yourself my FRIEND? If you were REALLY my friend, you wouldn't WANT to put me through all this pain again!"

Phyllis: "I **don't** want to, Elizabeth; I **am** your friend. I just don't know any other way to try to change someone's mind except to talk with them. If you can give me another way, I'll do that instead, most willingly."

Eliz.: "You're NOT going to give up, ARE you??"

Phyllis: "I hope not. I hope I have backbone enough not to."

Eliz.:   [Sighs.] "Oh, all right, Phyllis, go ahead and get it
          over with! But I warn you—you can't change my
          mind."
Phyllis: "Maybe not, but at least I will have tried."

Phyllis has taken three steps forward here. She has begun her discussion neutrally, instead of with a barrage of hostile words. She hasn't been ordered to leave, and Elizabeth has agreed to listen. This gives her the chance to make her case; it gives her a chance to maintain her role as friend rather than enemy. No matter what happens next, this is an improvement.

As always, it's critically important that when Phyllis says all these things she is careful to keep them free of hostile *intonation*. They already contain many very personal words and phrases; if they're spoken with extra emphatic stresses, set to negative tunes, they become hostile language that will serve no better than any other hostile language.

Now, suppose Phyllis goes ahead to present her case to Elizabeth, being very careful not to do any Blaming or Placating. Suppose she is careful not to give her friend any direct orders. Suppose she's careful to think of what she's doing as *building an agreement,* not *fighting a battle,* so that she can keep a clear head as she talks; that way, she's not likely to use any VAPs or other open hostilities. Suppose she puts her whole heart into her task and does it well—and that Elizabeth listens. What if Elizabeth then proceeds as in the original version B, using the metaphor *a house filled with chronic verbal abuse is a toxic waste dump,* reinforcing it with her statements about current scientific research? Elizabeth is saying, "I am like a woman who, living in a place filled with polluted food and water and toxic chemicals, must take urgent and extreme action to save her children from those dangers, both present and future." If that happens, what can Phyllis do?

There's one thing she should not do, because it will throw away any progress she's made up to that point. It will be no use at all for her to say, "That's not FAIR!" and accuse Elizabeth of trying to put her in a trap. We saw how that would end, with a panicked flight. And it will be no use for her to say anything in the "You're wrong because you're arguing with **me**!" style, unless she is prepared to handle something like this:

Phyllis: "I don't **care** if verbal abuse is as dangerous as all those other poisons! If you get a divorce, **you're wrong**, and that's all there is **to** it!"

Eliz.:   "Why? I'll listen while you explain that to me."

If Phyllis *can* explain it, she should. Either convincing Elizabeth that a verbally abusive home is not dangerous or, alternatively, convincing her that even if it is, breaking up that home is not a choice a Christian is free to make, might change her mind. If Elizabeth can convince Phyllis that her metaphor does hold true, she might be able to change *Phyllis's* mind. But even if neither mind is changed, this process of reasoning together instead of doing battle would almost surely end with the option of further discussion still open. This, too, is an improvement.

Finally, what if Phyllis can't explain? What if she has a gut feeling that the logical problem Elizabeth has posed is irrelevant, that the research must be flawed, and that the metaphor doesn't hold—but she doesn't know how to make that clear? Then it's time for her to say something like this:

Phyllis: "Elizabeth, I can't answer your question—I'm not wise enough to do that off the top of my head. But I feel like I **could** answer it, if you'll give me some time to think about it, and then let me come talk to you again."

Except when you find yourself up against a deadline with literally only minutes to spare, there's never anything wrong with admitting that you're not prepared to finish the discussion right then but are willing to *become* prepared and return for another try. What matters is keeping the lines of communication open, as shown above.

Workout Section

1. When I teach verbal self-defense, people often ask me for "a list of specific things to say [*or not to say*] to verbally abusive people." They're very disappointed when I tell them that no set of magic formulas exists. I can, however, tell them about a few small adjustments that have surprisingly large effects. One of those is something I call "Hedge-Clipping."

Hedges are patterns that speakers use to try to cancel—*in advance*—the probable consequences of their message. For example: "I know this is a stupid question, but . . ." and "You know I'd never tell you what to do, but. . . ." When we hear people say these things, we don't even want to listen to what comes next; our reaction is "If you KNOW that, then don't SAY it!" Hedges are irritating; they should be used only when they can't be avoided. We saw Phyllis avoiding a Hedge when she said, "I wish you could have said yes; I'm sorry you didn't feel that you could. And now I'm asking you to forgive me. . . ." The more likely wording would have been "But now I'm asking you to forgive me. . . ." Substituting "and" for "but" is one form of Hedge-Clipping. Here's another:

Don't say:
"I know this is a stupid question, but I have to ask it."
Instead, say:
"I know this is a stupid question. I'm sorry I have to ask it."

Here's a list of sentences that need Hedge-Clipping; rewrite them without the Hedges, so that they're less infuriating.

- "I **know** you don't want me to say this to you, but I just **have** to."
- "I **know** you're going to think this is crazy, but wait till you hear what **hap**pened."
- "I **know** you're too busy to listen to this, but it will only take a couple of **min**utes."
- "I know you told me not to talk about this ever **again,** but I **promise** this is the last time!"
- "I **know** you think it's okay to **do** that, but you're **wrong.**"
- "I **know** you think you can get **away** with that, but you're in for a real surprise!"
- "I **know** you think I owe you an apology, but let me tell you why that's not **true.**"

2. Here are three dialogues in which speakers feel obligated to raise objections on moral grounds, with the goal of persuading others to change their behavior. As we did for Scenario Ten, analyze the language to find the strategic errors, and then revise it to repair the damage and make a successful outcome more likely. You would also find it useful (and good practice in applying Miller's Law) to rewrite each dialogue *twice,* once from the viewpoint of each side in the argument.

Dialogue One

Phil: "Look, I **know** how **tough** this is for you, but I can't just step aside and let you do something **so** stupid and **so** wrong! Even YOU ought to have brains enough to know that you don't end a marriage over NOTHing!"

Art: "NOTHING? What do you MEAN, 'nothing'??!"

Phil: "So she told a few little **lies**! You don't divorce a woman for lying! **Can't** you **see** that—"

Art: "**Listen,** Phil! I know you think you're being a good friend here, but you're WAY out of LINE! I don't want to hear another word OUT of you! Understand?"

Phil: "But—"

Art: "NOT ANOTHER WORD!"

Dialogue Two

Lee: "Hey, **you** know how I am! The **last** thing I'd ever do is spoil everybody's **fun,** right? But I just wish there was **some** way I could make you understand that casino gambling is **wrong!** Not that I want to **preach** at you. . . . **I'm** no saint, you **know**? But—"

Carl: "Lee, **we** don't want to listen to that! If you don't want to go with us, **fine!** Don't **go!**"

Lee: "You mean you'd go **anyway,** knowing how I **feel about it**? How could you **do** that? Don't you even **care** if—"

Carl: "Lee . . . you're wasting your breath! You want to be a **prude,** that's your privilege! We'll see you later!"

Dialogue Three

Jane: "Sorry, but I can't go along with it. Don't ask."

Max: "Oh, come on, Jane. . . . There's no **way** any of us can make a decent living unless we can start selling drinks in our restaurants! We **need** your **support** on this! All you have to **do** is sign the **letter,** for crying out loud!"

Jane: "Max, people around here don't approve of alcohol; that's why it's a dry county. And I agree with them. Drinking is wicked."

Max: "If you had KIDS to support like the REST of us, you wouldn't SAY that! But YOU don't need the money! As long as YOU'RE okay, never MIND what happens to

US! You call that loving your NEIGHBOR? You could at
LEAST let me give you the REASONS why we feel
that—"

Jane: "I'm not interested in your reasons. And I suggest that
you behave like DECENT people and DROP this project!
It's WRONG, and you KNOW it is! Just give it UP!"

THOUGHT BITES

1. "People can seriously misunderstand what it is they're not saying to each other" (Rosenthal, "On Language," 1984).

2. "The driving force behind hostility is a cynical mistrust of others. Expecting that others will mistreat us, we are on the look-out for their bad behavior—and we can usually find it" (Williams, "Curing Type A," 1989, 26).

3. "A speaker . . . has to solve the problem: 'Given that I want to bring about such-and-such a result in the hearer's con-sciousness, what is the best way to accomplish this aim by using language?'" (Renkema, *Discourse Studies,* 1993, 97).

4. "Language is like a game, we are often told; but if so, it is a game with soft rules; not like chess, played on a board of abstract geometry, but rather like golf, to be played on this actual course or that" (Vendler, "Review," 1980, 209).

This is a useful metaphor for understanding how we make one grammar serve us for an infinite multitude of possible interac-tions. Language is a lot like golf, where—once you've learned how to swing the club, which club to use, and the like—you can use that knowledge on any golf course whatsoever. The "golf course" in a language interaction is the circumstances in which it takes place, your knowledge about the speaker, and similar fac-tors that will vary from one situation to another.

5. "Christian theology affirms and celebrates the power of language, and especially the power of the spoken word. Language is the medium through which we relate to one another and to God" [Cunningham, *Faithful Persuasion*, 1990, 36].

CONCLUSION

The fruit of the Spirit is love, joy, peace, long-suffering, kindness, goodness, faithfulness, gentleness, self-control.
Galatians 5:22–23

Notice that the verse does not say the fruit of the Spirit is control over others, but *self*-control. It does not say that the fruit of the Spirit is victory and triumph. Neither winning nor losing is mentioned; but joy is, and peace.

At the beginning of this book I suggested to you that the people who ask me all those questions about how on earth they can turn the other cheek in today's world are asking the *wrong* questions. I suggested that when they tell me the task is impossible, or possible only for saints, they are right. But not because the commandment itself is impossible for ordinary human beings to obey—that could only mean that God can't be trusted. Rather, the task is impossible because it is the wrong task. They are trying to do something they were never told to do.

The fault is not that they are flawed in their character or their intelligence or their faith, not that they are weak or hypocritical, but that they have misunderstood the meaning of the message. Winning—which they understand to be their obligation because they are following the Warrior metaphor's rules—is utterly foreign to the meaning of "turn the other cheek." They are like a man who is distraught when he finds himself unable to play tennis with a fishing rod and concludes that it has to be because something is wrong with *him*. He would cry out in despair, "How am I supposed to hit that ball with this skinny little metal **rod**? It's im**pos**sible!" And the response would be: "Nobody ever asked you to do that. You haven't failed; you've just misunderstood."

The *right* questions to ask are these three:

1. How can I learn to speak to others, and to understand when others speak to me, in such a way that hostility and violence are set aside even when we disagree, and winning and losing are irrelevant?

2. How can I gain **access** to the information about language that is already my birthright, so that I will know beyond question that I can trust myself to answer whatever language comes my way? That when I make mistakes in my communication I will always know how to go about setting them right?

3. How can I become aware of the resources of my language, so that I have many choices in disagreements and can be sure that violence in my communication with others will always be my **last** resort, chosen with reluctance and sorrow?

Some of the answers to those questions are in this book, which you have now read and worked through with me. Not *all* of the answers, of course! But *enough* of them so that you now know how to look for additional answers with confidence and skill.

You have learned a set of basic linguistic techniques that make it possible for you to avoid hostile language in your own speech and react to the hostile language of others with rational detachment and forbearance. Most of the information about those techniques was already stored in your internal grammar, in your long-term memory, but you had no reliable or systematic access to it. Now you do! The set includes:

True listening, aided by Miller's Law

This is the foundation and the cornerstone for good communication. Unless you listen to others with your full attention and give courteous consideration to their perceptions, communication is impossible, and your other language skills are useless to you. Without true listening, you will hear hostility and hostile motivations where none exist, and you will base your behavior upon those phantoms.

Proper use of the sensory modes

People become less skilled with language and more restricted in their linguistic choices when they are tense and under stress. No communication is more stressful than that which takes place between two people who speak different languages; communication with differing sensory modes is a much smaller problem, but it is a problem of the same kind. When people are in distress, it helps tremendously for you to speak to them in the vocabulary of their dominant sensory system. It reduces the tension and increases the understanding of everyone involved.

Proper use of the Satir Modes

Because human language is an interactive feedback loop, when hostility is introduced by one speaker and the response is more hostility, a *hostility loop* is created. The more it is fed, the more it will grow and the stronger it will become. When you make your Satir Mode choices with this in mind, you are able to avoid setting up hostility loops yourself, and you know how to see to it—gently—that others' attempts to set them up always fail.

Three-part messages for criticism—both negative and positive—and for commands

When people are distracted by their automatic negative reaction to criticism and commands, they aren't able to listen; without listening, they cannot understand what is being asked of them or what comment is being made about them. Three-part messages give you a way around that automatic negative reaction.

Proper management of the English verbal attack patterns

The English verbal attack patterns, which guarantee verbal combat, are a set of ritualized scripts that have become a *habit*, used without thought. They are a linguistic reflection of the Warrior metaphor, imposing the "win or lose" rule in every case, no matter how trivial or absurd. They waste a tremendous amount of our time and energy, and they create havoc. Because they require the participation of both attacker and target, they're easily managed: You simply refrain from flinging VAPs at others, and you refuse to take the bait in VAPs that others fling at you. Those measures come easily to you when you understand that people who use VAPs almost never do so to cause pain, but because they desperately need attention, or because they are unaware that better methods for dealing with conflict exist.

Proper understanding of metaphors and the process of metaphor

A metaphor such as "My God is a mighty fortress" is a tool for understanding and speaking about God and fortresses in terms of those features that the two have in common. "A human being is a mammal," though very similar in its structure, is not a metaphor but a statement of a fact about human beings. Because you use metaphors as your primary mechanism for filtering and organizing your perceptions and for making decisions about much of your behavior, your understanding of two points is critical.

First, you need to understand that metaphors are *not* statements of fact. Second, you need to understand that you are free to *choose* among metaphors. This, together with respect for the extraordinary *power* of metaphors, is all that is necessary.

By using the set of techniques above, you reduce to an absolute minimum the number of times in your life when turning the other cheek requires you to call upon your reserves of faith and moral strength. Those will be rare—instead of being a constant, incessant, intolerable burden in your life.

You know now that you *can* achieve this goal. Only one issue remains: *Is it ethical and moral to use the techniques of language that make it possible?* I will keep my promise and answer that question now; I am happy to be able to tell you that the answer is *yes*.

People usually state this concern to me in two parts:

1. When we use those techniques, aren't we being **manipulative?**
2. Won't people who learn those techniques just use them to verbally **abuse** others more skillfully?

The first question is easily answered. The whole concept of "manipulative" communication is based on the myth that *neutral* communication is possible. It isn't. I can't say anything to you without having as my goals at least that you will stop talking while I'm speaking and that you will listen to what I say. There's no reason for me to talk to you unless I have those two goals and am prepared to pursue them. "Manipulation" is *built in* to the communication process in the same way that oxygen is built in to the process of breathing. Infants and tiny children accomplish it by screaming at the top of their lungs, while older humans ordinarily learn less primitive methods—but we all do it, and we cannot do otherwise. Since we *must* manipulate, it's far better for us to know what we are doing and how to do it *well*.

The other question worried me when I first began teaching this system. I really was concerned that verbal abusers might learn it for the single purpose of becoming more highly *skilled* verbal abusers. But after a quarter century, I am confident when I tell you that it doesn't happen. A sadist will collect and master a tool for causing pain, whether it is a butcher knife or a cruel sentence. I can't keep sadists from using what I teach, any more than I can keep them from using butcher knives. But sadists are terribly sick and mercifully rare; we cannot use them as an excuse to remain ignorant of the miraculous resources of our language.

Stop and think. When have you ever read a paper or listened to a newscast and learned that someone with a black belt in a martial art had gone out and started beating people up? *People who know absolutely that they are fully capable of handling whatever may come at them from others have no need to throw their weight around and no interest in doing so.* The more capable they are of injuring others, the less likely they are to use that ability, and the more scrupulously they avoid any situation with even the slightest *hint* of abuse. The same thing is true, for normal human beings, of being highly skilled in the art of verbal self-defense. All true martial arts are *gentle* arts; this one is no exception. You need not worry that just because you know far more about how to cause pain with language than you did before, you will suddenly be tempted to act that out—it does not happen.

Welcome to a world in which you can say to the bully and the blusterer and the poor soul who knows no nonviolent way to talk: "Notice, I am not afraid of you at all"—and mean it with all your heart.

References
and
Bibliography

Articles

1. Addington, D. W. "The Relationship of Selected Vocal Characteristics to Personality Perception." *Speech Monographs* 35 (1968): 492–503.
2. Bell, C. "Family Violence." *Journal of the American Medical Association* (19 September 1986): 1501–1502.
3. Blanck, Peter D. "The Appearance of Justine: Judges' Verbal and Nonverbal Behavior in Criminal Jury Trials." *Stanford Law Review* (November 1985): 89–163.
4. Briggs, David. "U.S. Bishops: Wives Need Not Submit to Abusive Husbands." *Laconia (New Hampshire) Citizen* (October 30, 1992).
5. Easwaran, Ekmath. "Three Harmonies." *Parabola* (Winter 1991): 48–55.
6. Everett, William Johnson. "Sunday Monarchists and Monday Citizens." *The Christian Century*, 503–505.
7. Ferguson, John. "The Crux of the Matter." *Fellowship* (March/April 1980): 10–11, 19.
8. Gibbs, Nancy. "The EQ Factor." *Time*, 2 October 1995, 60–68.
9. Griffin, William. "Tony Campolo: Partying with God." *Publishers Weekly*, 6 September 1991, 36–38.
10. Hall, Elizabeth. "Giving Away Psychology in the 80s: George Miller Interviewed by Elizabeth Hall." *Psychology Today*, January 1980, 38–50, 97–98.
11. Hamill, Pete. "End Game." *Esquire*, December 1994, 85–92.

12. Hollien, M. "Vocal Indicators of Psychological Stress." *Annals of the New York Academy of Science* 347 (1980): 47–72.
13. "Image and Likeness." *Parabola*, Spring 1985, 62–71.
14. Lakoff, George. "Metaphor & War." *East Bay Express*, 22 February 1991, 1–2, 18–19.
15. Lapham, Lewis H. "Notebook: Entr'acte." *Harper's*, October 1995, 7–9.
16. Lynch, James J. "Listen and Live." *American Health*, April 1985, 39–43.
17. —. "Interpersonal Aspects of Blood Pressure Control." *Journal of Nervous and Mental Diseases* 170 (1982): 143–153.
18. Milstead, Janie. "Verbal Battering." *BBW Magazine*, August 1985, 34–35, 61, 68.
19. Nelson, J. Robert. "Genetics and Theology: A Complementarity?" *The Christian Century*, 20 April, 1988, 388–389.
20. Neuhaus, Richard John. "Why We Can Get Along." *First Things* (February 1996): 27–34.
21. Novak, Michael. "Of War and Justice." *Forbes*, 4 March 1991, 58.
22. —. "A New View of Man: How Christianity Has Changed Political Economy." *Imprimis*, May 1995, 1–7.
23. O'Reilly, Mary Rose. "Deep Listening." *Friends Journal*, November 1994, 16–17.
24. Rosenthal, Jack. "On Language." *New York Times Magazine*, 15 July 1984.
25. Seligman, J., et al. "Emotional Child Abuse: Discipline's Fine Line." *Newsweek*, 3 October 1988, 48–50.
26. —. "The Wounds of Words: When Verbal Abuse Is as Scary as Physical Abuse." *Newsweek*, 12 October 1992, 90–92.
27. Shea, M. J. "Mental Stress and the Heart." *Cardiovascular Reviews & Reports*, April 1988, 51–58.
28. Sheler, Jeffery L. "Holy War Doctrine." *U.S. News & World Report*, 11 February 1991, 55–56.
29. Steel, Ronald. "Let Them Sink." *The New Republic*, 2 November 1992, 15–16.
30. Telushkin, Rabbi Joseph. "Words That Hurt, Words That Heal: How to Choose Words Wisely and Well." *Imprimis*, January 1996, 2.
31. Terrell, Richard. "Just How Good Is Contemporary Christian Literature?" *Christianity and the Arts*, August/November 1996, 7–10.

32. Ury, William. "Getting Past No." *Management Digest*, February 1991, 12–13.

33. Vendler, Zeno. "Review of Peter Cole, *Syntax & Semantics*, Vol. 90." *Language*, March 1980, 209–214.

34. Wael, J. M. "Unlearning Skepticism: An Angelic Meditation." *The Christian Century*, 28 September 1988, 827–828.

35. Waldrop, M. Mitchell. "The Trillion-Dollar Vision of Dee Hock." *Fast Company*, October/November 1996, 75–86.

36. Williams, Redford. "Curing Type A: The Trusting Heart." *New Age Journal*, May/June 1989, 26–30, 101.

37. Woodbridge, John D. "Culture War Casualties." *Christianity Today*, 6 March 1995, 20–26.

38. Wright, H. Norman. "Toxic Talk." *Christian Parenting Today*, July/August 1991, 24–30.

BOOKS

1. Bellah, Robert H., et al. 1985. *Habits of the Heart: Individualism and Commitment in American Life*. New York: Harper & Row.

2. Blumenthal, M. D., et al. 1975. *More about Justifying Violence: Methodological Studies of Attitudes and Behavior*. Ann Arbor: University of Michigan Press.

3. Bolton, Robert. 1979. *People Skills: How to Assert Yourself, Listen to Others, and Resolve Conflicts*. Englewood Cliffs, N.J.: Prentice Hall.

4. Cloud, Dr. Henry. 1992. *Changes That Heal: How to Understand Your Past to Ensure a Healthier Future*. New York: Zondervan/Harper-Collins.

5. Cunningham, David S. 1990. *Faithful Persuasion: In Aid of a Rhetoric of Christian Theology*. Notre Dame: University of Notre Dame Press.

6. Dillard, Annie. 1979. *Holy the Firm*. New York: Bantam/Harper & Row.

7. Elgin, Suzette Haden. 1979. *What Is Linguistics?* 2nd ed. Englewood Cliffs, N.J.: Prentice Hall.

8. —. 1983. *More on the Gentle Art of Verbal Self-Defense*. New York: Prentice Hall.

9. —. 1985. *The Gentle Art of Verbal Self-Defense*. New York: Barnes & Noble. (Originally published by Prentice Hall, 1980.)

10. —. 1987. *The Last Word on the Gentle Art of Verbal Self-Defense.* Englewood Cliffs, N.J.: Prentice Hall. (Reissued by Barnes & Noble, New York, 1996.)

11. —. 1989. *Success with the Gentle Art of Verbal Self-Defense.* Englewood Cliffs, N.J.: Prentice Hall.

12. —. 1989b. *Mastering the Gentle Art of Verbal Self-Defense.* (Audio program.) Englewood Cliffs, N.J.: Prentice Hall.

13. —. 1991. *Staying Well with the Gentle Art of Verbal Self-Defense.* Englewood Cliffs, N.J.: Prentice Hall. (Reissued by MJF Publications, New York, 1996.)

14. —. 1994. *GenderSpeak: Men, Women, and the Gentle Art of Verbal Self-Defense.* New York: John Wiley.

15. —. 1995. *BusinessSpeak.* New York: McGrawHill.

16. —. 1995. *"You Can't Say That To Me!": Stopping the Pain of Verbal Abuse—An 8-Step Program.* New York: John Wiley.

17. —. 1996. *The Gentle Art of Communicating with Kids.* New York: John Wiley.

18. —. 1997. *Try to Feel It My Way: New Help for Touch Dominant People and Those Who Care About Them.* New York: John Wiley.

19. —. 1997b. *How to Disagree Without Being Disagreeable: Getting Your Point Across with the Gentle Art of Verbal Self-Defense.* New York: John Wiley.

20. Gordon, Dr. Thomas. 1977. *Leader Effectiveness Training.* New York: Wyden Books.

21. Graham, Dom Aelred. 1971. *The End of Religion: Autobiographical Explorations.* New York: Harcourt Brace.

22. Johnston, Elizabeth A. 1993. *She Who Is: The Mystery of God in Feminist Discourse.* New York: Crossroads.

23. Lakoff, George, and Mark Johnson. 1980. *Metaphors We Live By.* Chicago: University of Chicago Press.

24. Lechman, Judith C. 1987. *The Spirituality of Gentleness: Growing Toward Christian Wholeness.* San Francisco: Harper & Row.

25. Lewis, C. D. 1987. *Inspirational Writings of C. S. Lewis.* New York: Inspirational Press.

26. Lynch, James J. 1977. *The Broken Heart: The Medical Consequences of Loneliness.* New York: Basic Books.

27. —. 1985. *The Language of the Heart: The Body's Response to Human Dialogue.* New York: Basic Books.

28. Mendell, Adrienne, M.A. 1996. *How Men Think: The Seven Essential Rules for Making It in a Man's World*. New York: Fawcett Columbine.

29. Minirth, Dr. Frank, Dr. Brian Newman, and Dr. Paul Warren. 1992. *The Father Book*. Nashville: Thomas Nelson.

30. Montagu, Ashley. 1986. *Touching: The Human Significance of the Skin*. New York: Harper & Row.

31. Navrone, John, S.J. 1990. *Seeking God in Story*. Collegeville, Minn: The Liturgical Press.

32. Oates, Wayne E. 1973. *The Psychology of Religion*. Waco, Tex.: Word Books.

33. Ornstein, Robert, and David Sobel. 1978. *The Healing Brain: Breakthrough Discoveries About How the Brain Keeps Us Healthy*. New York: Simon & Schuster.

34. Owens, Virginia Stem. 1995. *Daughters of Eve: Women of the Bible Speak to Women of Today*. Colorado Springs: NavPress Publishing.

35. Palmer, Earl F. 1986. *The Enormous Exception: Meeting Christ in the Sermon on the Mount*. Waco, Tex.: Word Books.

36. Peale, Norman Vincent. 1961. *The Power of Positive Thinking*. Englewood Cliffs, N.J: Prentice Hall.

37. Peck, M. Scott, M.D. 1978. *The Road Less Traveled: A New Psychology of Love, Traditional Values and Spiritual Growth*. New York: Simon & Schuster.

38. Regan, Augustine. 1979. *Thou Shalt Not Kill*. Butler, Wis.: Clergy Book Service.

39. Renkema, Jan. 1993. *Discourse Studies: An Introductory Textbook*. Philadelphia: John Benjamins.

40. Satir, Virginia. 1964. *Conjoint Family Therapy*. Palo Alto, Calif.: Science & Behavior Books.

41. ——. 1972. *Peoplemaking*. Palo Alto, Calif: Science & Behavior Books.

42. Spence, Gerry. 1995. *How to Argue and Win Every Time*. New York: St. Martins.

43. Urner, Carol Reilley. 1994. *The Kingdom and the Way: Meditations on the Kingdom of God*. (Pendle Hill Pamphlet 317) Wallingford, Penn.: Pendle Hill Publications.

44. Watts, Alan. 1971. *Does It Matter?* New York: Vintage Books.

45. Watzlawick, Paul, et al. 1967. *Pragmatics of Human Communication: A Study of Interactional Patterns, Pathologies, and Paradoxes.* New York: Norton.
46. Weber, Stu. 1993. *Tender Warrior.* Sisters, Oreg.: Multnomah Books/Questar.
47. Wren, Brian. 1991. *What Language Shall I Borrow? God Talk in Worship: A Male Response to Feminist Theology.* New York: Crossroad.

INDEX

ABOUT THE AUTHOR

Dr. Suzette Haden Elgin, who holds a doctorate degree in linguistics, is the author of the best-selling book *The Gentle Art of Verbal Self Defense*. She has been leading seminars in communication nationwide for more than twenty years, as well as teaching at every level of the educational system. She also maintains a private practice as a communications consultant.